African perspectives on
China in Africa

Books published by Fahamu

Firoze Manji and Patrick Burnett (eds) (2005) *African Voices on Development and Social Justice: editorials from Pambazuka News 2004*. Dar es Salaam: Mkuki na Nyota Publishers. ISBN-10: 9987-417-35-3

Roselynn Musa, Faiza Jama Mohammed and Firoze Manji (eds) (2006) *Breathing Life into the African Union Protocol on Women's Rights in Africa*. Nairobi and Addis Ababa: SOAWR and the African Union Commission Directorate of Women, Gender and Development. ISBN-13: 978-1-9-4855-66-8 (also available in French: ISBN-13: 978-1-904855-68-2)

Patrick Burnett, Shereen Karmali and Firoze Manji (eds) (2007) *Grace, Tenacity and Eloquence: The Struggle for Women's Rights in Africa*. Nairobi and Oxford: Fahamu and SOAWR. ISBN-13: 978-0-9545637-2-1

Firoze Manji and Stephen Marks (eds) (2007) *African Perspectives on China in Africa*. Nairobi and Oxford: Fahamu. ISBN-13: 978-0-9545637-3-8

African perspectives on
China in Africa

Edited by
Firoze Manji
and Stephen Marks

PAMBAZUKA

First published 2007 by Fahamu – Networks for Social Justice
Cape Town, Nairobi and Oxford
www.fahamu.org
www.pambazuka.org

Fahamu, 2nd floor, 51 Cornmarket Street, Oxford OX1 3HA, UK

Fahamu South Africa, The Studio, 6 Cromer Road,
Muizenberg 7945, Cape Town, South Africa

Fahamu Kenya, PO Box 47158, 00100 GPO, Nairobi, Kenya

British Library Cataloguing in Publication Data
A catalogue record for this book is available from the British Library

ISBN: 978-0-9545637-3-8

Cover illustration and design by Judith Charlton, Fahamu
The characters on the cover are Chinese for Africa

CONTENTS

ACKNOWLEDGEMENTS

This publication was made possible with the help of grants from Christian Aid and TrustAfrica, to whom go our sincere thanks. Our thanks, too, are due to the authors, who delivered to impossible deadlines. Thanks must also go to Shereen Karmali for project management and copyediting, Stephanie Kitchen for help with copyediting, Judith Charlton for design and layout, Naomi Robertson for proofreading, and to Patrick Burnett and Mandisi Majavu, who helped to produce the special issue of Pambazuka News (no 282 of 14 November 2006) (www.pambazuka.org).

PREFACE

FIROZE MANJI

2006 was the 50th anniversary of the establishment of the first diplomatic ties between China and African countries and saw an increased focus on the relationship between China and Africa. In June 2006, Chinese President Hu Jintao and Premier Wen Jiabao visited ten African countries to promote China–Africa relations. In November, African heads of state met in Beijing to learn of a massive Chinese package of aid and assistance, including preferential loans, cancellation of debts, and numerous other initatives.

China's involvement in Africa has provoked much debate and discussion. Is China just the latest in a line of exploiters of Africa's rich natural resources who put their own economic interests above humanitarian, environmental or human rights concerns, or is China's engagement an extension of 'South–South solidarity'? Does China's engagement enable African countries to free themselves from the tyranny of debt and conditionality that, through two decades of structural adjustment programmes, have reversed most of the gains of independence, or is Africa just swapping one tyranny for another?

Much of the commentary on China in Africa focuses either on assessing how Western capital's interest might be affected, or on denouncing China for practices that have for centuries been the norm for US and European powers – support for dictators, callous destruction of the environment, exploitation of minerals, and complete disregard for human rights. Lost in the cacophony has been the voice of independent African analysts and activists, which you can hear in this collection of essays. As these articles demonstrate, there is no single 'African view' about China in Africa, but the authors are united by their concern for, and commitment to, social justice for Africa's people.

Historically, China has played a different role in Africa from Africa's colonial powers, supporting African countries in various liberation struggles, providing educational opportunities and assisting in healthcare. Moreover, the rise of China in Africa does not just make problems for the continent, it also creates opportunities. As Stephen Marks pointed out in a recent editorial in Pambazuka News, Western corporations and governments now face competition – there is an alternative to the dictates of the international financial institutions – and this can give African states more room for manoeuvre. The African Union as well as civil society need to consider how to react to China's challenge while avoiding 'uncritical acceptance on the one hand or mere rejectionism on the other'.

With the support of Christian Aid and TrustAfrica, Fahamu undertook a work in progress to identify leading institutions, activists and academics within Africa who were working on China. In the course of this review, we commissioned a number of researchers to write papers on the key issues for both a special issue of Pambazuka News (issue 282 of 14 December 2006) and this book. Given the relatively short deadlines available to ensure that the book would be available at the World Social Forum, not everyone we approached was able to respond. The articles in this book provide, therefore, only a taste of the richness of research and reflection on the subject of China's emerging role in Africa.

Our intention in publishing this book is both to reflect the current thinking on the subject as well as to help nurture further research and engagement. But in so doing, we know that we are only beginning to understand the shifts in the balance of forces in Africa that are emerging as a result of what some refer to as 'South–South cooperation'. There are four other players whose role needs further attention: India, Venezuela, Brazil and South Africa. We hope to turn our attention to these 'new' players in the coming year.

Firoze Manji is director of Fahamu and editor of Pambazuka News.

If capitalism is restored in a big socialist country, it will inevitably become a superpower. The Great Proletarian Cultural Revolution, which has been carried out in China in recent years, and the campaign of criticizing Lin Piao and Confucius now under way throughout China, are both aimed at preventing capitalist restoration and ensuring that socialist China will never change her colour but will always stand by the oppressed peoples and oppressed nations.

If one day China should change her colour and turn into a superpower, if she too should play the tyrant in the world, and everywhere subject others to her bullying, aggression and exploitation, the people of the world should identify her as social-imperialism, expose it, oppose it and work together with the Chinese people to overthrow it.

Deng Xiaoping
Speech at special session of the UN General Assembly, 1974

INTRODUCTION

STEPHEN MARKS

Stephen Marks introduces the articles in this publication by reviewing the billion-dollar glamour on display in Beijing during a summit between African and Chinese leaders in early November 2006. But behind the glitz, what does it all mean for Africa? Is it colonialism revisited, a mad dash for African oil and minerals? Is there a Chinese model of development that can be followed? And what is the true nature of Chinese involvement in Africa?

Heads of state and dignitaries from 48 countries flocked to Beijing in November 2006 to attend the largest international summit ever held in the Chinese capital. And China pulled out all the stops, not only, or not even, to make the VIP guests feel welcome, but also to leave China's people and the world at large in no doubt of the meeting's importance.

Bright red banners lined the streets with slogans lauding 'Friendship, Peace, Cooperation and Development.' China's official news agency Xinhua declared that the visitors 'brought a trend of the mysterious continent to the capital of China'.[1] Giraffes and elephants frolicking on the savannahs were spread over giant billboards on all the capital's main streets and squares.

'The CDs and DVDs on Africa are very popular, and some of the African musical products have been sold out,' Xinhua reported a shop assistant as saying. And 'In a restaurant of African food in the Chaoyang District, east of Beijing, it's hard to find a seat in the recent week. The unique foods and hot African dances attracted many people.'

But behind the official 'Africa chic' and the predictable warm words of the official communiqués, something substantial was going on. The declaration adopted at the end of the meeting on Sunday 5 November was strong on 'motherhood and apple pie' rhetoric, promising 'a new type of strategic partnership' founded on 'political equality and mutual trust, economic win-win cooperation and cultural exchanges'. But there was impressive substance too.

On Saturday 4 November, China's Premier Wen Jiabao proposed that China and Africa should seek to bring their trade volume to US$100 billion by 2010. This would more than double the 2005 level, about US$39.7 billion. In the first nine months of this year, China–Africa trade had already surged to US$40.6 billion, up 42 per cent year-on-year.

On the same day China's President Hu Jintao announced a package of aid and assistance measures to Africa including US$3 billion of preferential loans in the next three years and the cancellation of more debt owed by poor African countries. China, he pledged, would:

- Double its 2006 assistance to Africa by 2009
- Provide US$3 billion of preferential loans and US$2 billion of preferential buyer's credits to Africa in the next three years
- Set up a China–Africa development fund, which would reach US$5 billion, to encourage Chinese companies to invest in Africa and provide support to them
- Cancel debt in the form of all the interest-free government loans that matured at the end of 2005 owed by the heavily indebted poor countries and the least developed countries in Africa that have diplomatic relations with China
- Increase from 190 to over 440 the number of export items to China receiving zero-tariff treatment from the least developed countries in Africa with diplomatic ties with China.
- Establish three to five trade and economic cooperation zones in Africa in the next three years
- Over the next three years, train 15,000 African professionals; send 100 senior agricultural experts to Africa; set up 10 special agricultural technology demonstration centres in Africa; build 30 hospitals in Africa and provide a grant of RMB 300 million for providing artemisinin[2] and build 30 malaria prevention and treatment centres to fight malaria in Africa; dispatch 300 youth volunteers to Africa; build 100 rural schools in Africa; and increase the number of Chinese government scholarships to African students from the current 2,000 per year to 4,000 per year by 2009.

President Hu even pledged to build a conference centre for the African Union 'to support African countries in their efforts to strengthen themselves through unity and support the process of African integration' – perhaps a visible reinforcement of the final statement's pledge to support 'the African regional and sub-regional organisations in their efforts to promote economic integration, and [support] the African countries in implementing the "New Partnership for Africa's Development" programs'.

Early on Sunday morning, the 2nd Conference of Chinese and African Entrepreneurs concluded with 14 agreements signed between 11 Chinese enterprises and African governments and firms, worth a total of US$1.9 bil-

> *Perhaps the material distinction is not between Chinese capital and Western, but rather between the merely rapacious, and the more sophisticated.*

lion. The agreements cover cooperation in infrastructure facilities, communications, technology and equipment, energy and resources development, finance and insurance.

The biggest deal was one worth US$938m, for China's state-owned Citic conglomerate, to set up an aluminium plant in Egypt. There was also a new copper project, worth US$200m, in Zambia, along with plans to build a US$55m cement factory in Cape Verde. A mining contract with South Africa, worth US$230m, was also announced.

There was more good news to come. The summit was followed by a two-day African Trade Fair in Beijing. According to Xinhua 'Over 170 enterprises from 23 African countries filled a Beijing exhibition hall on Monday with varieties of their local specialties, including minerals, jewelry, textile, fur, spice, tea and coffee.'

Zhao Jinping, deputy director of the foreign economy department under the State Council Development and Research Centre, told Xinhua that the summit's decisions 'offers Chinese private firms unprecedented opportunities to invest in Africa'.

But except for textiles, which are notoriously hard-hit by Chinese exports, all the items listed as on display were primary products which Africa was already exporting in colonial times. Perhaps this influenced Xinhua's choice of Chinese entrepreneurs to interview on their view of future business prospects in Africa.

'Wang Jianping, president of the Hashan Company in eastern Zhejiang

---

one aspect of the 'Chinese model' which is certainly appealing to Africa's more repressive regimes is the idea that it represents a refutation of the view that democracy is an essential precondition for development

---

Province, told Xinhua that after the summit, he decided to increase investment in Nigeria from two million dollars to six million dollars so as to boost the development of local shoemaking industry.'

'Sheng Jushan, general manager of the Guoji Group in central China's Henan Province, said his company has just set up an economic cooperation zone in Sierra Leone, which attracts about 20 Chinese small and medium-sized enterprises.'

A similar processing zone in Nigeria, according to Xinhua, 'when completed and put into operation, will help boost economic activities in the state through processing local raw materials into manufactured goods, especially those that have to be imported now in the country'.

Colonialism revisited?

China's race for Africa is certainly due in large part to the same causes as Europe's 19th century scramble – the need for raw materials to fuel industrialisation. As *The Economist* summarised it before the summit:

Its economy has grown by an average of 9% a year over the past ten years, and foreign trade has increased fivefold. It needs stuff of all sorts—minerals, farm products, timber and oil, oil, oil. China alone was responsible for 40% of the global increase in oil demand between 2000 and 2004.

The resulting commodity prices have been good for most of Africa. Higher prices combined with higher production have helped local economies. Sub-Saharan Africa's real GDP increased by an average of 4.4% in 2001-04, compared with 2.6% in the previous three years. Africa's economy grew by 5.5% in 2005 and is expected to do even better this year and next.[3]

In Beijing in 2005 Moeletsi Mbeki, deputy chairman of the South African Institute of International Affairs, spelled out to a conference organised by the Chinese Parliament what many feared might be the result:

Africa sells raw materials to China and China sells manufactured products to Africa. This is a dangerous equation that reproduces Africa's old relationship with colonial powers. The equation is not sustainable for a number of reasons. First Africa needs to preserve its natural resources to use in the future for its own industrialisation. Secondly China's export strategy is contributing to the de-industrialisation of some middle-income countries ... it is in the interests of both Africa and China to find solutions to these strategies.[4]

Clearly, many of the decisions announced at the summit reflect Chinese awareness of these fears of a 'new imperialism'.[5] So did the *People's Daily* article before the summit indignantly denouncing 'The fallacy that China is exercising "neo-colonialism" in Africa' which was 'apparently aimed at sowing discord between China and Africa'.[6]

And on the eve of the summit the state council, China's cabinet, issued 'Nine Principles' to 'Encourage and Standardise Enterprises' Overseas Investment'. The principles require Chinese companies operating overseas to 'abide by local laws, bid contracts on the basis of transparency and equality, protect the labor rights of local employees, protect the environment, implement corporate responsibilities and so on'.[7]

Reviewing the issues

Clearly, to respond to the challenge of China's turn to Africa, activists will need to situate its actions against the background of its original source in China's raw material needs, as John Rocha does in his article. They will also need to keep abreast of the detailed impact of China's operations on the ground, including those cases where the rape of natural resources and the impact of infrastructure developments on land rights and on the environment is at its most destructive, and is most reminiscent of traditional colonialism – as Anabela Lemos and Daniel Ribeiro do in their report on Mozambique, and as Ali Askouri does in reviewing the impact of Chinese investment in Sudan.

China's close links with Robert Mugabe, which he at least boosts as a model of the concept of 'win–win economic cooperation' deserves special attention, which John Karumbidza gives it here. And the nature of China's development aid also needs analysis and comparison with others, as Moreblessings Chidaushe bring to bear.

Work in all these areas will need to continue; and Daniel Large's critique of the idea of 'Chinese exceptionalism' should provide it with a sound foundation. But, as Michelle Chan-Fishel points out, Chinese companies in their operations in Africa and at home, appear to repeat the same environmentally and socially destructive model already exemplified by the West. A host of further question marks will therefore be raised over the widespread concept that China's own development path has lessons for Africa – an 'alternative Chinese way'.

Is there a Chinese model?

The most obvious answer to the question is 'yes' in the sense that, like Japan and the smaller 'Asian tigers', China did not develop by following the rules of the Washington consensus. Critical attention in the West and also in Africa, has been focused on China's avoidance of good governance and human rights conditionality now commonly insisted on by the West, and this undoubtedly lies behind much of the enthusiasm for the 'Chinese model' on the part of Africa's more repressive regimes.

But there is also substance to the idea that 'South–South' cooperation has merit in its own right. In areas such as rural development and intermediate technology China's experience does indeed have much to offer that is of greater relevance precisely because China too is a developing country.

As John Rocha points out in his article, codes such as the African Peer Review Mechanism were not intended to be part of an aid conditionality package, and the perception that they are externally imposed has damaged their reputation even in the eyes of campaigners and activists who support their objectives.

Conversely, China's avoidance of conditionality means that she can move faster to produce visible results on the ground. The statism which still characterises China's economy means that China can offer a 'one-stop shop' approach, in which contracts guaranteeing China its desired access to oil or key minerals, as in Angola, or Nigeria, can be combined with soft loans and much-needed infrastructure projects such as highways and railways, and low-cost, high-impact 'add-ons' such as rural development projects, industrial parks for small firms, and training and scholarships.

Thus the BBC reported on 28 April 2006:

Chinese President Hu Jintao has signed an important oil exploration agreement with Kenya during his trip to Nairobi. Six other deals have also been signed on malaria, rice and roads. Mr Hu is also due to visit wildlife parks that are eager to attract Chinese tourists. Kenya is keen to secure Chinese investment deals in the pharmaceutical and technology sectors.

...The president's trip has focussed on deals to expand Chinese investment in Africa's natural resources, especially oil, to satisfy China's energy-hungry economy.

On Wednesday, China secured four oil drilling licences from Nigeria in a deal involving $4bn in investment.

The deals cover:
* Road maintenance in Nairobi
* Support for rice-growing schemes
* Maintenance of a sports centre
* Setting up an anti-malaria health centre.[8]

It could also be pointed out that before 1949 some of the main obstacles to China's development were to be found in chronic national disunity and warlordism on a scale whose closest parallel in today's Africa is the Democratic Republic of Congo.

This integrated approach can be a genuine plus-point, and not only for such regimes as those in Zimbabwe or Sudan. As in this example, the whole deal can be tied up and delivered in visits by top governmental figures, reciprocated by red-carpet treatment for African leaders, as at the recent Beijing summit.

But not all these factors are unique to China, and future analysis would benefit by looking at China's approach in a wider context, rather than in the one-track contrast with the conventional model of liberal globalisation which characterises conventional Western approaches.

As Chris Melvile and Molly Owen have pointed out[9] China is not the only player in the 'South–South' game, or the only one to promote the idea as offering 'win-win' benefits. India, Brazil and South Africa have established their own 'south-south' links. Each has also been welcomed as an alternative to the old imperialist powers. And each in its turn has been accused of pursuing its own 'sub-imperialist' agenda.

And as Chris Alden and Martyn Davies point out:

Chinese MNCs (multinational corporations) are in many respects like other MNCs operating in Africa, for example France's Elf-Aquitaine or South Africa's Eskom. In the French case, Elf-Aquitaine has been highly politicised, building up or even defining France's Africa policy in particular countries such as Gabon or Angola.

The close proximity between French business and political interests manifested by the presence of oil company executives in the inner circle at the Elysee Palace as well as the circulation of key political elites such as Jean-Christophe Mitterrand within political and business circles, has been a feature of France's post-independence African policy from the outset.

Moreover the modus operandi of foreign policy makers in Paris has been to construct policy around a network of personal relationships with individual African leaders, bolstered by a web of bilateral agreements in trade, finance, development assistance and defence.[10]

The nature of the Chinese multinational corporations

If the role of the Chinese state is not so different to that of at least some Western and 'Southern' states, how does the Chinese MNC itself differ from its rivals in the way in which it operates as a firm?

China's government made its position clear in its official policy statement on Africa; 'The Chinese Government encourages and supports Chinese enterprises' investment and business in Africa, and will continue to provide preferential loans and buyer credits to this end.'[11]

As Mark Sorbara puts it: 'Investing in African extractive industries is a risky business, but China is desperately in need of raw materials to feed its booming economy, hence the government is willing to shoulder most of the risk for Chinese companies looking to invest in Africa'.[12]

But the purpose of this state backing is not only to secure China's access to raw materials. As Alden and Davies point out:

> In pursuit of its broader global ambitions, Beijing is intent on 'picking corporate champions' that, with the benefit of active and generous support from the state, are being groomed to join the ranks of the Fortune 500. Roughly 180 companies have been designated by the state to benefit from preferential finance, tax concessions and political backing to 'go global' and become true multinationals.[13]

This aim to be global players in their own right was made clear by Fu Chengyu, chief executive of China's oil giant CNOOC after the US Congress moved to block CNOOC's takeover bid for Unocal, the US' ninth-largest oil firm: 'We aim to be a participant in the global industry, like all the international majors, supplying the global marketplace as well.'[14]

The same seems to apply to the China–South Africa deal, concluded at the Beijing summit, to set up a joint company to expand ferro-chrome production in South Africa. Reuters' report on the deal commented that 'China has become a big investor in mining and natural resources in Africa as it seeks the raw materials to feed its economic growth, but unlike many Sino-African deals the purpose of Tubatse Chrome is to make money rather than to supply metal to China'. And the chairman of the South African partner was quoted as saying: 'Sinosteel is a trading organisation, and Tubatse Chrome will be a profit-driven company. If China offers the best price we will sell it to China, but we will sell to wherever we can get the best price.'[15]

Optimists may view this as a good sign. As Ndubisi Obiorah puts it:

> As Chinese companies move up the global pecking order and discover the considerable mark-up to be derived from possessing premium brands and intellectual property, they will seek to establish their own brands. As global branding and reputation become more important to Chinese companies, they may become less willing to be associated with human rights abuses and repressive regimes in Africa and elsewhere.[16]

As a result, he suggests, Chinese companies could become more vulnerable to 'naming and shaming' from NGOs in Western countries and elswhere.

Optimists may also see some signs of this on the websites of Sinopec and Petrochina, which feature prominently their awards for corporate governance, and their 'model' policies on health, safety and environmental protection.

Does this establish the need for a 'corporate China watch' to be set up, for activists in Africa and elsewhere to bring this pressure to bear? But in that case why single out China? As Alden and Davies conclude: 'Indeed even critics admit that if one sets aside the particular cases of Sudan, Angola and Equatorial Guinea, "the rest of PetroChina and Sinopec activities on the African continent are not especially reprehensible" or at least no more so than many of their Western counterparts.'[17]

Perhaps the material distinction is not between Chinese capital and

Western, but rather between the merely rapacious, and the more sophisti-cated. Even these are not two separate categories, but at least as much two different faces, each of which may be presented as convenient.

In this context, those involved in corporate research could usefully exam-ine the possibility that Chinese MNCs operating in Africa might themselves incorporate some Western capital, perhaps percolating not only through the obvious channel of joint ventures and shareholdings, but also through funds from Hong Kong and Taiwan.

Neil Tottman, head of commercial banking at HSBC China, has laid out aggressive plans for its commercial banking businesses in China, in anticipa-tion of further deregulation of the sector this year. 'The total volume of busi-ness referrals between Hong Kong and the mainland grew at an annual rate of 175 percent between 2002 and 2005. This year to date, volume between Taiwan and the mainland has increased 512 percent over the same period last year.'[18]

The anti-democratic road?

But there is one other aspect of the concept of a distinctive 'Chinese model' which is certainly appealing to Africa's more repressive regimes – the idea that it represents a refutation of the view that democracy is an essential pre-condition for development. The view is widely held that China proves the opposite - the need for strong government.

Ndubisi Obiorah quotes a Nigerian example of this invocation of a 'Chinese model': 'leading lights of the Obasanjo faction claimed that an absence of sta-bility and visionary leadership were the principal cause of Africa's underde-velopment and that it was these same qualities that had enabled Singapore and China to become contemporary economic miracles'.[19]

As Obiorah points out, the rise of India might counter this self-interested vogue for authoritarian government. It could also be pointed out that before 1949 some of the main obstacles to China's development were to be found in the close ties of ruling elites to forces at home and abroad opposed to modernisation; in archaic patterns of land ownership and authority; and in chronic national disunity and warlordism on a scale whose closest parallel in today's Africa is the Democratic Republic of Congo (DRC). All of these were swept away by a massive popular revolution – a prospect likely to be at least as unacceptable to Africa's current repressive elites as a more gradual and reformist path to democratisation.

But the most powerful antidote to the idea that China validates an authoritarian road to development is the growing grassroots unrest in China over the cost of the country's current economic model in its impact on employment rights, the environment and mounting inequality and social exclusion.

As Dorothy Guerrero has pointed out:

> China is now the world's fourth-largest economy and many developing countries envy its record of economic progress. However, China's phenomenal growth is producing a big misconception in that it is viewed as a big winner of globalisation.
>
> Although it is true that market reforms and China's opening to the global economy gave millions of people there an increased standard of living, more Chinese people are suffering the consequences of its rapid transition to a market-based economy.
>
> The majority of the Chinese people are not too concerned about when China will become the world's largest economy. Rather, they are asking, 'When will the benefits of China's rise to superpower status start to affect our lives positively?'[20]

Even official sources in China and abroad are aware of the social costs of China's free-market great leap forward. Members of the legislature have warned of the country's impending employment crisis[21] and the World Bank has confirmed that China's poor are getting poorer.[22]

As for the environment, no less a figure than Pan Yue, deputy director of China's State Environmental Protection Administration, sparked controversy with a recent essay *On Socialist Ecological Civilisation* when he openly charged that: 'The economic and environmental inequalities caused by a flawed understanding of growth and political achievement, held by some officials, have gone against the basic aims of socialism and abandoned the achievements of Chinese socialism.'[23]

The march of neoliberalism within China and its impact on the Chinese people has advanced hand-in-hand with China's growing imperialist role abroad.[24] This apparent anomaly of an imperialist power itself subject to growing imperialist exploitation in alliance with local capital is not new – it also characterised Czarist Russia. And difficult though it may currently seem to act on the idea, the connection suggests that an obvious grassroots ally of activist and civil society groups in Africa will increasingly be their opposite numbers in China itself.[25]

Stephen Marks is a freelance researcher, writer and consultant specialising in issues of economic development, human rights, planning, and the environment.

Notes

1 For all references to official documents and speeches at the November summit, and to Xinhua coverage of it, see the official summit website at http://english.focacsummit.org/

2 A drug extracted from a shrub in Chinese traditional medicine and used to treat malaria.

3 *The Economist* (2006) 'Never too late to scramble', 26 Oct <http://www.economist.com/world/africa/displaystory.cfm?story_id=8089719>.

4 M. Mbeki (2006) *South African Journal of International Affairs*, 13(1):7.

5 Stephen Marks (2006) 'China in Africa - the new imperialism?', *Pambazuka News*, 244, 2 March <http://www.pambazuka.org/en/category/features/32432>.

6 People's Daily Online (2006) 20 October <http://english.people.com.cn/200610/30/eng20061030_316577.html>

7 Scott Zhou (2006) 'China as Africa's angel in white', *Asia Times*, 3 November <http://www.atimes.com/atimes/China_Business/HK03Cb04.html>.

8 BBC (2006) 28 April <http://news.bbc.co.uk/2/hi/africa/4953588.stm>.

9 Chris Melville and Olly Owen (2005) 'China and Africa: a new era of "south-south cooperation"', Open Democracy, 8 July <http://www.opendemocracy.net/globalization-G8/south_2658.jsp>.

10 Chris Alden and Martyn Davies (2006) 'A profile of the operation of Chinese multinationals in Africa', *South African Journal of International Affairs*, 13(1):84.

11 http://english.people.com.cn/200601/12/eng20060112_234894.html.

12 Mark Sobara (2006) *The Nation*, Nairobi, 14 April, quoted by Yang Lihua in 'Africa; a view from China', *South African Journal of International Affairs*, 13(1).

13 Alden and Davies (2006).

14 Quoted by Alden and Davies (2006), 91.

15 Reuters South Africa (2006) 'Samancor signs China chrome deals', 9 November <http://za.today.reuters.com/news/newsArticle.aspx?type=businessNews&storyID=2006-11-

09T062122Z_01_BAN922845_RTRIDST_0_OZABS-MINERALS-CHROME-SAMANCOR-20061109.XML>

16 Leni Wild and David Mepham (eds) (2006) *The New Sinosphere: China in Africa*, Institute for Public Policy Research, 51.

17 Alden and Davies (2006) 95.

18 China View (2006) 'HSBC banks on sustained growth', 17 October <http://news.xinhuanet.com/english/2006-10/17/content_5212967.htm>.

19 Leni Wild and David Mepham (2006).

20 Dorothy Guerrero (2006) 'China: beyond the growth figures', *The Globalist*, 21 February <2006http://www.theglobalist.com/DBWeb/printStoryId.aspx?StoryId=5095 >

21 People's Daily Online (2006) 'China facing employment crisis with 34.5 mln new job-seekers in next five years' <http://english.people.com.cn/200610/16/print20061016_312247.html>

22 Richard McGregor (2006) 'China's poorest worse off after boom', *Financial Times*, 12 November <http://www.ft.com/cms/s/e28495ce-7988-11db-b257-0000779e2340.html>.

23 Pan Yue and Zhou Jigang (2006) 'The rich consume and the poor suffer the pollution', Chinadialogue, 27 October <http://www.chinadialogue.net/article/show/single/en/493--The-rich-consume-and-the-poor-suffer-the-pollution-?page=1#disscuss-bara%20chinese%20ecosocialist?>.

24 Peter Kwong (2006) 'China and the US are joined at the hip: the Chinese face of neoliberalism', *Counterpunch*, 7/8 October <http://www.counterpunch.org/kwong10072006.html>.

25 Sophie Beach (2006) 'China's New Left calls for a social alternative – Pankaj Mishra', China Digital Times, 13 October <http://chinadigitaltimes.net/2006/10/chinas_new_left_calls_for_a_social_alternative_pankaj_m.php>.

A NEW FRONTIER IN THE EXPLOITATION OF AFRICA'S NATURAL RESOURCES: THE EMERGENCE OF CHINA

JOHN ROCHA

John Rocha sets out to answer two questions related to China's role in Africa: To what extent will China's growing influence in Africa either advance or undermine the African agenda? And what are the challenges and implications that these hold for African governments, the private sector and the international community?

Providing an expansive overview of China's interests in Africa, Rocha examines both the positive and negative implications for Africa and the meaning of China's involvement for NEPAD's African Peer Review Mechanism.

Introduction

China's burgeoning influence around the globe has captured the attention of governments, the private sector and civil society. With a large population and recent high economic growth rates, estimated at 9.5 per cent, China now comes only second to the United States of America (USA) in its consumption of oil. Based on current projections, Chinese demand for and consumption of mineral resources is expected to grow exponentially in the foreseeable future, so in an attempt to diversify its source of supply, China has set its sights on Africa as a natural partner.

While this development is certainly welcomed by many African states, in international circles it has prompted some analysts to postulate that China's Africa strategy is largely underpinned by its voracious appetite for natural resources, especially gas, oil and minerals rather than a genuine desire to foster strong and long-lasting partnerships with Africa. Linked to this is a growing concern that China's rising influence in Africa could derail international attempts to foster good governance in Africa. The argument is that because China does not insist on commitment to democracy, good governance and respect for human rights as a precondition for development assistance, Western pressure to that effect is diluted.

Others argue that stronger cooperation with Africa could also increase China's sphere of influence and bolster its attempts to redefine its relation to the rest of the world. This would be a dramatic change in the traditional

---

There is also a growing realisation that traditional relations and partnerships with the West have not helped Africa overcome the structural obstacles to eradicating poverty and reversing its economic marginalisation.

---

patterns of Western dominance over African affairs and would diminish Western political and economic leverage over the continent, thereby constituting a major challenge to Western hegemony over the political, economic and development discourse in Africa and internationally.

With this in mind, the main purpose of this paper is to provide an African perspective on the ongoing debate about China's role in Africa by contextualizing this evolution within the African development agenda as represented by the African Union and the New Partnership for Africa's Development (NEPAD). In particular, special attention is given to the following questions: To what extent would China's growing influence in Africa either advance or undermine the African development agenda? What challenges and implications do these hold for African governments, the private sector and the international community? The paper also sheds some light on how African governments and the international community, including the private sector, should respond to some of these challenges.

16

Background and context

Within Africa towards the beginning of the 21st century, African leaders adopted NEPAD and transformed the erstwhile Organisation of African Unity (OAU) into a more vibrant African Union (AU). The need to end the continued marginalisation of Africa and reverse the development chasm between Africa and the rest of the world was a core objective. From China's viewpoint, it was adopting the prevailing global strategy aimed at opening opportunities for foreign investment in China as well as creating new markets for Chinese investments abroad. A key feature of both initiatives is an ardent desire to improve South–South relations in order to strengthen the role of developing countries in international affairs.

Notwithstanding the international communities' commitment to double total overseas development assistance to Africa by an additional US$25 billion by 2010, the composition, scale and slow pace of delivery is generating a certain level of disillusionment with Africa's traditional development partners. There is also a growing realisation that traditional relations and partnerships with the West have not helped Africa overcome the structural obstacles to eradicating poverty and reversing its economic marginalisation. Rather than develop, Africa is haemorrhaging while the rest of the world accumulates wealth at its expense through the unbalanced exploitation of its natural resources and the enforcement of a distorted international economic system. Logically, strengthened cooperation with China is seen as a way of addressing some of these structural imbalances.

Current status and trends in China–Africa cooperation

According to the Chinese Ministry of Land and Natural Resources, there were 158 minerals with identified resources and reserves in China in 2004. However, these resources are insufficient to meet an ever-increasing domestic demand and to sustain China's dramatic economic growth. For instance, based on projections by the Ministry of Land and Natural Resources, by 2010 domestic crude oil production will be able to meet 51–55 per cent of demand and only 34–40 per cent by 2020; while domestic iron production will be able to meet 38 per cent of demand by 2010 and only 29 per cent by

2020. It is estimated that by 2010 and 2020 the shortage of coal will reach 250 million and 700 million tons respectively.[1] So China is looking to Africa to address some of its short- to long-term needs.

Historically, the availability of cheap raw materials and the prospects for huge returns on investments, particularly from the exploitation of natural resources, has always provided an incentive for the expansion and deepening of political and economic ties with Africa. Africa is blessed with an impressive endowment of mineral wealth, including near-global monopolies of platinum, chromium and diamonds; a high proportion of the world's

---

the availability of cheap
raw materials and the prospects
for huge returns on investments
has always provided an incentive
for the expansion and deepening
of political and economic
ties with Africa

---

gold, cobalt and manganese reserves; and extensive reserves of bauxite, coal, uranium, copper and nickel (see Table 1). Of the proved oil reserves currently estimated, Africa accounts for 7 per cent of the global total.[2] New oil discoveries have been made in Madagascar, Zambia and Uganda while extensive exploration is ongoing in Ethiopia, Kenya and Tanzania. It is estimated that by 2010, the Gulf of Guinea will contribute at least one out of every five new barrels onto the global market. The bulk of this will come from Angola and Nigeria followed by others (see Table 2). Africa also has substantial quantities of the world's remaining natural gas reserves (see Table 3). It is this capacity that endears Africa to China and the rest of the world. Both the Addis Ababa Action Plan 2004–2006 and the China Africa Policy emphasise the need to intensify cooperation on natural resources exploration under the principle of mutual, beneficial, reciprocal and sustainable development.

Table 1 Africa's mineral reserves versus world reserves

Commodity	Africa (reserves)	World (reserves)	Africa relative to world (%)
Platinum group metals (t)	63,000	71,000	89
Diamonds (million carats)	350	580	60
Cobalt (t)	3,690,000	7,000,000	53
Zirconium (t)	14	38	37
Gold (t)	10,059	35,941	28
Vanadium (t)	3,000,000	13,000,000	23
Uranium (t)	656	4,416	15
Manganese (kt)	52,000	380,000	14
Chromium (1000t)	100,000	810,000	12
Titanium (kt)	63,000	660,000	10
Nickel (kt)	4,205	62,000	7
Coal (mt)	55,367	984,453	6

Source: Presentation by Mr Sam Jonah, former president of AngloGold Ashanti, University of South Africa, 2005

Table 2 Oil production in sub-Saharan Africa by 2010 (in thousands of barrels/day)

Country	2000	2005	2010
Nigeria	2,040	2,555	3,500
Angola	750	1,100	2,050
Chad	0	35	390
São Tomé & Principe	0	25	350
Equatorial Guinea	118	350	350
Congo (Brazzaville)	283	222	197
Gabon	271	204	134
Cameroon	116	72	68
Côte d'Ivoire	7	55	85
DRC	25	35	28
Mauritania	0	0	125
Guinea Bissau	0	0	250
Total	3,610	4,866	7,527

Source: The Africa Report, March 2006

Table 3 Proved natural gas reserves

Country	Natural gas (trillion cubic feet) BP Statistical Review Year end 2004	Natural gas (trillion cubic feet) CEDIGAZ 1-Jan-05	Natural gas (trillion cubic feet) Oil & Gas Journal 1-Jan-06	Natural gas (trillion cubic feet) World oil Year end 2004
Algeria	160.439	161.743	160.505	171.5
Angola		13.067	1.62	4
Benin		0	0.04	
Cameroon		3.496	3.9	
Congo (Brazzaville)		4.061	3.2	4.15
Congo (Kinshasa)		0	0.035	
Cote d'Ivoire (Ivory Coast)		0.918	1	
Djibouti	0	0	0	0
Egypt	65.452	66.004	58.5	66
Equatorial Guinea		2.472	1.3	3.4
Ethiopia		0.883	0.88	
Gabon		1.059	1.2	3.425
Ghana		0.848	0.84	
Libya	52.632	51.313	52.65	51.5
Morocco			0.06	
Mozambique		2.19	4.5	0
Namibia		2.472	2.2	0
Nigeria	176.394	178.517	184.66	180
Rwanda		2.013	2	
Somalia		0.212	0.2	

South Africa		0.353	0.001	
Sudan		3.037	3	4
Tanzania		0.989	0.8	
Tunisia		2.649	2.75	3.885
Other-Country Not Specified	41.513	0.177	Not applicable	8.899
Africa total	**496.43**	**498.86**	**485.841**	**500.759**

Source: US Energy Information Administration

Currently, China derives a quarter of its oil imports from Africa through its oil interests in Algeria, Angola, Chad, Sudan and increasing stakes in Equatorial Guinea, Gabon and Nigeria.[3] Oil exploration rights were established in Sudan in 1995 by the China National Petroleum Corporation (CNPC) through ownership of a 40 per cent stake in the Greater Nile Petroleum Operating Company where it is pumping over 300,000 barrels per day. Another Chinese firm, Sinopec, is constructing a 1,500-kilometre (932 miles) pipeline to Port Sudan on the Red Sea, where China's Petroleum Engineering Construction Group is building a tanker terminal. China has invested more than US$8 billion worth of oil exploration contracts in the Sudan.[4] In Nigeria, the China National Offshore Oil Corporation (CNOOC) acquired a 45 per cent working interest in an offshore oil mining licence, OML 130, for US$2.268 billion cash; CNPC invested in the Port Harcourt refinery[5] while Petro-China is interested in the Kaduna refinery. ONGC Mittal Energy Ltd (OMEL), the joint venture between the Oil and Natural Gas Corporation and the L. N. Mittal Group, will invest US$6 billion in railways, oil refining and power in exchange for oil drilling rights.

Similar investments have been made in Gabon by Sinopec and Unipec through a joint venture with Total while Pan-Ocean exploits the Tsiengui on-shore basin and is associated with Shell to explore Awokou-1.[6] Gabon is now selling one-fifth of its annual oil output to China.

Another deal that has attracted the attention of the international community is the US$2 billion Chinese–Angolan cooperation agreements.[7] It is reported that the value of this has since risen to almost U$9 billion. The general agreements focus particularly on enhancing Chinese–Angolan cooperation in the oil and gas as well as mineral resources sectors. Three definite oil agreements were signed whereby Sonangol, Angola's state oil company agreed to supply oil to China's Sinopec oil company. This was supplemented by agreements for Sonangol and Sinopec to jointly evaluate Angola's offshore Block 3 as well to study plans for the development of a new oil refinery in Angola. In addition, the agreements also foresee cooperation between the Angolan Ministries of Petroleum and Geology and Mining and China's National Commission for Development and Reform, focusing on technical aid.

While Chinese oil deals have captured the attention of the world, much less is being said about China's demand for the main base metals such as aluminium, copper, iron ore, nickel, zinc and other minerals. In the DRC, Feza Mining, a joint venture between the Chinese company Wambao Resources Corporation and some Congolese businessmen, is finishing a pyrometallurgic plant which, according to the DRC's Ministry of Mines, should produce 1,000 tonnes of pure cobalt per year. In Zambia, China has invested nearly $170 million in the mining sector, focusing primarily but not only on copper.[8] China is to build a US$200 million copper smelter at Zambia's Chambeshi Mine with a capacity to produce 150,000 tons a year. In Gabon, a Chinese consortium headed by the China National Machinery and Equipment Import and Export Corporation (CEMEC) has been granted sole rights to exploit huge untapped iron ore reserves and build the costly rail links needed to reach them in the tropical forest. This has been at the expense of the world's leading iron miner, Vale do Rio Doce (CVRD).[9]

Over the past decade, China's imports in all major primary commodity categories, except ores and metals, grew significantly more rapidly from Africa than from the world as a whole.[10] China also sources over 20 per cent of its log imports from Africa while China is the destination of about 13 per cent of Africa's log exports. Overall, Africa's share of the most dynamic primary commodities in China's imports has also risen substantially during this period (see Table 4 and Figure 1).

Table 4 Share of Africa in China's total imports, by major commodity groups, 1994–2003 (in percentages)

	1994	1996	1998	2000	2002	2003	Change in absolute value (1994–2003) (per cent)	
							Total imports	Imports from Africa
Total primary commodities	2.6	3.4	3.1	8.8	7.6	8.1	362	1348
Agricultural raw materials	3.2	4.4	4.3	4.3	4.4	5.4	214	437
Fuels	1.7	4.0	3.7	17.3	15.1	16.4	622	6976
Ores and metals	5.4	4.8	3.7	3.7	4.1	3.6	495	299

Source: COMTRADE

Figure 1 China's primary imports from world and from Africa, by major commodity groups, average annual rate of growth, 1994–2003 (percentages)

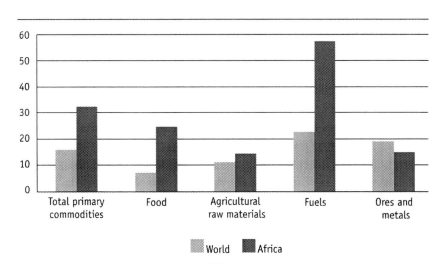

Source: COMTRADE and estimates by UNCTAD

Features of Chinese investments in Africa

China's approach to Africa has several distinct characteristics. For example, a key feature of Chinese cooperation with Africa is the strong links between the Chinese government's foreign policy objectives and the role played by Chinese enterprises. By the end of June 2003, the Chinese Ministry of Commerce had given approval to 602 Chinese enterprises to invest a total of US$1.173 billion in Africa. This had risen to 715 by the end of 2004.[11] The range of activities that these companies are engaged in varies from trade, processing, manufacture, communication, transportation, roads and agriculture, to resources development.

For example in Angola, the US$2bn deal has lead to the rebuilding of national roads, the building of a new airport in the outskirts of Luanda and other major infrastructure development projects. In addition, a US$69 million agreement was signed between Angola's MundoStartel and China's ZTE Corporation and the Angolan Council of Ministers approved broader ZTE operations. These which will see ZTE invest US$400 million, of which US$300 million will be used to modernise and expand Angola Telekom to develop telephone networks in Angola. According to the Angolan government, the remaining US$100 million is to be invested in military communications, the development of a mobile telephone factory and the creation of a telecommunications training institute for Angolan employees.[12] It is the multifaceted character of Chinese involvement in Africa that seems to be a major draw for African countries.

On a positive note, there is no doubt that Chinese investments in Africa are having and could continue to have some positive impacts. China is helping African countries to rebuild their infrastructure and providing other types of assistance to agriculture, water, health, education and other sectors. This could have very positive spin-offs in lowering transaction costs and assisting African governments to address social calamities such as poor health services, energy crisis, skills development, etc. Increased Chinese demand for raw materials has seen an upsurge in commodity prices, putting extra cash in the coffers of many resource-dependent economies. However, African countries should use this windfall to make provision for the future by investing heavily in education and training, diversifying the economy and strengthening the administrative and governance systems – political, economic and corporate – in order to be better able to maintain and sustain the current economic boom throughout the continent.

On a pessimistic note, the NEPAD framework extols the virtues of African self-reliance, ownership and leadership as well as good economic, political and corporate governance as the bedrock of its development agenda. The emergence of China as a key player in Africa could undermine the NEPAD vision since it could make African countries increasingly reliant on China rather than on their own domestic resources and the resourcefulness of their people. At present, China and not NEPAD or the domestic market is being seen as a more reliable source for resource mobilisation. There are also concerns about Chinese funded projects where in some cases, the ratio of Chinese expatriates (labour and enterprises) to locals contracted is as high as 70 per cent Chinese and 30 per cent local. This practice does not help Africa in addressing the problems of high unemployment and the scourge of poverty. Nor does it assist Africa's private sector to grow both technically and financially. Instead it could entrench African dependence on external assistance.

The governance conundrum

At the beginning of the 21st century, Africa's leaders adopted NEPAD and transformed the OAU into the AU. Underpinning these initiatives are concrete commitments to transforming the nature of governance throughout the continent to ensure that good political, economic and corporate governance prevails. The African Peer Review Mechanism (APRM) was adopted to deliver this commitment and to date 25 countries have acceded to it. In July 2002, the AU summit adopted the Declaration on Democracy, Political, Economic and Corporate Governance, which recognises 'good economic and corporate governance including transparency in financial management as essential pre-requisites for promoting economic growth and reducing poverty'. Yet, again despite calls by NEPAD for untied aid, accession to the APRM is being used by some sectors of the international community as a condition for receiving aid. This practice is undermining the credibility of the entire NEPAD process, including the APRM as many countries now regard the APRM as being an external instrument.

The international community has notably invested a lot of effort and resources in advocacy and other initiatives to foster good governance in Africa's natural resources sector. The Kimberley Process, the Extractive Industries Transparency Initiative (EITI), Publish What You Pay and various other codes and standards have been discussed and adopted at various forums. So far, only Cameroon, the Republic of Congo, the Democratic Republic of Congo, Gabon, Ghana, Guinea, Mauritania, Nigeria, São Tomé and Príncipe and Sierra Leone have implemented the EITI principles.

The remaining 41 countries, including some of the most stable democracies in the continent such as Botswana, Namibia and South Africa, have kept their distance. However, even in the countries where progress has already

---

The emergence of China as a key player in Africa could undermine the NEPAD vision since it could make African countries increasingly reliant on China rather than on their own domestic resources and the resourcefulness of their people.

---

been made the pace is sluggish, requiring, in some instances, a certain degree of coercion. The underlying motive for this lethargic approach is that the EITI lacks the necessary political legitimacy within the continent since it was developed outside and is largely externally driven. The same applies to the other initiatives, which are largely ad-hoc and sector specific.

The emergence of China has raised fears that China's non-adherence to the West's approach of imposing aid conditionalities has the potential to nullify all the progress made in fighting corruption and improving governance in Africa – implying that the problem of corruption in Africa is solely an African problem. There is a one-dimensional focus on Africa as the source of the problem whilst ignoring its global character. This brings us to the broader debate on capital flight. While it is correct that the revenue pilfered from Africa by its elites represents a major challenge to the economic growth and sustainable development of the continent, the haemorrhaging of money away from the continent also takes place in other forms. According to Raymond Baker, a renowned researcher on these matters, mispricing and transfer pricing are some of the tricks used to move money out of developing countries.

At this juncture, it is useful to refer to the UN Convention against Corruption, which entered into force on 14 December 2005. So far 29 African countries have ratified it whilst several of Africa's major trading partners, including China, have also acceded. Article 5 (1) states that 'each State Party shall, in accordance with the fundamental principles of its legal system, develop and implement or maintain effective, coordinated anti-corruption policies that promote the participation of society and reflect the principles of the rule of law, proper management of public affairs and public property, integrity, transparency and accountability'. Paragraph 2 goes further and states that 'each State party shall endeavour to establish and promote effective practices aimed at the prevention of corruption'.

With regard to the private sector, Article 12 (3) of the convention explicitly extols state parties to:

> take such a measures as may be necessary, in accordance with its domestic laws and regulations regarding the maintenance of books and records, financial statement disclosures and accounting and auditing standards, to prohibit the following acts carried out for the purposes of committing any offences established in accordance with this Convention:
> a) The establishment of off-the-books accounts;
> b) The making of off-the-books or inadequately identified transactions;
> c) The recording of non-existent expenditures;
> d) The entry into liabilities with incorrect identification of their objects;
> e) The use of false documents; and
> f) The intentional destruction of bookkeeping documents earlier than foreseen

Whereas initiatives such as the EITI and Publish What You Pay seek to address some aspects of the UN Convention, Article 10,[13] the narrow focus on transparency and accountability alone, while critical, is not enough. A core objective of the UN convention is to 'promote integrity, accountability and *proper management of public affairs and public property*' (emphasis added).[14] As it is currently constituted and marketed, the EITI is unclear on how it intends to deal with the issues raised in Article 12 (3) of the UN Convention against Corruption nor has it shown any inclination to align itself with existing domestic laws and instruments or even other continental instruments such as the APRM, AU Convention on Preventing and Combating Corruption or related instruments.

Further, in my view, the effective and efficient management of public revenue and assets should not be limited to the public declaration of the proceeds accrued by African governments from the exploitation of natural resources. It should also entail ensuring that these transactions produce optimal benefits to the African people. For instance, there are issues related to the repatriation of profits, mispricing[15] and transfer pricing,[16] which include but are not limited to the extractive industries. These practices are major contributors to increased corruption and have served as useful conduits for corrupt practices as well as capital flight. In addition, Africa is not only loosing money through corruption and other money laundering activities but it is also the victim of a distorted international economic system. These issues are not adequately addressed by the EITI and other initiatives proposed by the international community.

It would be in Africa's best interest to use the opportunity presented by the greater interest in the continent's natural resources to put in place adequate policies, laws, regulations and systems to effectively manage not only the act of extracting resources but also the manner in which the products of the extraction processes are managed. This should include the inflow and outflow of goods and capital so as to stem the continued undermining of the economic interests of African states, be it by China or any other interested parties.

Raising the stakes and the new scramble for Africa

The emergence of China as a dominant player in Africa raises two critical challenges for Africa and the international community. The first one pertains to Africa's weak administrative systems (poor revenue generation, management and disbursement capacity), the absence of the rule of law and heavy dependence on natural resources. This situation is compounded by the lack of adequately skilled personnel and technological know-how, all of which are necessary ingredients for translating Africa's natural resources into the development of the continent and its people. It is these acute weaknesses that make Africa susceptible to what is commonly known as the resources curse.

Second, it is abundantly clear that increased economic development over the next few decades, regardless of regional variations, will have a significant impact on increasing demand for vital resources. Consumption, in Africa as elsewhere, is bound to increase with improved standards of

> *The emergence of China has raised fears that its non-adherence to the West's approach of imposing aid conditionalities has the potential to nullify all the progress made in fighting corruption and improving governance in Africa – implying that the problem of corruption in Africa is solely an African problem.*

living. Consequently, the dynamics of increased economic growth and development, growing populations, increasing consumption and dwindling resources will generate intense competition over access and control of natural resources. The impact of these developments will be particularly severe in Africa given the acute weaknesses described above.

Africa is already a major supplier of raw materials to the European Union, United States and other developed countries and newcomers such as Brazil, India, South Korea and other emerging economies are joining these importing countries. This certainly elevates the strategic importance of Africa for the world economy. For example, in 2005 the EU purchased 36.4 per cent of sub-Saharan Africa's exports, with an estimated total of US$9.2 billion worth of minerals, while oil imports by the USA, amounting to US$40.1 billion and accounting for 79.8 per cent of all US purchases, continued to dominate imports from sub-Saharan Africa. Recently, riding on the back of China, South Korea also signed a US$10 billion rail-for-oil deal with Nigeria.[17]

In view of this, it would be dangerous to limit discussions to the narrow governance agenda of corruption and transparency. Instead, Africa and the international community should focus their attention on devising mutually beneficial strategies to address the common challenges confronting the world. There is a need for national, bilateral and multilateral mechanisms to manage the intricate web of interests that the increased competition over natural resources will generate. These mechanisms should ensure that competition for access and control of strategic natural resources does not degenerate into a climate in which the social, economic and political viability of African or any other states is undermined.

Within Africa, the continental mandate provided by the African Peace and Security Agenda (APSA) recognises the issue of resource exploitation as a key matter affecting peace, security and socio-economic development. This mandate also makes clear the need to delineate minimum standards for the management and exploitation of natural resources, particularly in areas affected by conflict. This mandate is based on the recognition that the manner in which natural resources are managed and exploited has the potential to either enhance and guarantee state and human security or undermine it. Consultation has started to develop these minimum standards .

The way forward

There is a general agreement that Africa's wide variety of natural resources could be an essential tool in the fight against poverty, underdevelopment and marginalisation. The recent discovery of oil in Madagascar, Zambia and Uganda also demonstrates that Africa's potential mineral resources are still a mystery to Africa and the world. Africa is a continent yet to be fully explored and its latent economic potential unleashed. However, there is a need for a paradigm shift on the part of Africa's leadership both within the public and private sectors. The community at large and civil society organisations are crucial in ensuring that Africa's natural resources are exploited and managed in a manner that contributes to the eradication of poverty as well as sustainable economic growth and development.

First, there is a need to place the broader national interest above short-term personal gain. In most African countries the state or the head of state are the custodians of natural resources on behalf of the people. The constitution enjoins them to exploit and manage these resources for the benefit of the nation. It is imperative that these constitutional provisions are strictly adhered to and implemented with vigour. The institutional, legislative, regulatory and enforcement capacity of the state must be strengthened so that it serves as a deterrent against unscrupulous and opportunistic behaviour. In order to ensure that Chinese or other multinational enterprises investing in Africa conduct their business in manner that enhances social cohesion and economic growth, the conduct of Africa's leaders, public institutions, businesses and citizens need to be exemplary and beyond reproach.

Second, there currently seems to be no clear regional or continental strategy to deal effectively with the myriad of actors. This is resulting in a fragmented approach which weakens Africa's bargaining position. In stark contrast, China and all the other actors are coming into Africa with well thought out and packaged proposals that enable them to maximise the benefits from any relationship with African countries. China, in particular, seems to have a purposeful strategy and is successfully delivering on all its objectives vis-à-vis Africa. The question is what is the driving force behind Africa's sudden economic interest in China? Is it part of a well-calculated approach to unlock the continent's true economic potential or is it merely a meek response to an unfolding development. Given Africa's experience with the West before and after independence, the English saying 'once bitten, twice shy'[18] is of particular relevance.

Further, while the super cycle of increasing demand for commodities and high prices is undoubtedly generating enormous benefits for African countries and is set to continue, the continent must guard against the Dutch Disease syndrome.[19] Diversifying its economy and export base should be a key priority for Africa. By developing secondary and tertiary industries Africa would generate additional employment opportunities, bolster revenue for the state and enhance economic growth. Despite its major contribution as a supplier of raw materials, Africa's development prospects are constrained by its heavy reliance on the primary sector as the dominant element in its economies. This situation is compounded by a distorted international system that facilitates the export of raw materials but inhibits and restricts the trade in processed goods from Africa. So far, China does not show any meaningful deviation from this well entrenched international practice.

However, as mentioned earlier, increasing international demand for commodities has resulted in a shift from a buyer's market to a seller's market. This is likely to continue for the foreseeable future, driven principally by the Asian boom under the leadership of China as well as India. Essentially, the emergence of new players provides an opportunity for resource endowed countries since they are now in a position of strength and spoilt for choice in trade negotiations.

This opportunity must be fully exploited and maximised if Africa is to extricate itself from the periphery and take centre stage in the global economy. For example, Africa must diversify its economy by identifying strategic niches and insisting on local beneficiation; negotiating better terms of trade at a bilateral and multilateral level as well as using its natural resources endowment as leverage in political and economic negotiations with international partners. However, for this to be effective Africa needs to adopt a more coordinated and integrated approach in its dealings, whether at bilateral or multilateral level. Unlike the Chinas and other major economies of this world that are backed up by strong political and economic clout, Africa's ability and capacity for leverage is rather limited.

There is also room for enhanced civil society cooperation across Africa. At present community participation in the exploitation and management of natural resources is rather limited. Where it happens, the conduct and practices employed by communities can sometimes be self-destructive, as with the *garimpeiros*[20] in Angola or the rebels in the Niger Delta. Another major opportunity for civil society is in the area of research and knowledge management. There is an information vacuum and this is having a negative impact on policy development and implementation.

The bottom-line is to ensure that the dialogue between the international community and Africa becomes more constructive and reinforces the NEPAD principles of partnership, mutual respect and benefit. The overarching objective of such a process should be to ensure that Africa's natural resources are managed in an effective and sustainable manner for the benefit of the continent and the global economy. In other words, continental and global sustainable peace, security, stability and sustainable development should constitute the pillars for future cooperation in this vital sector.

John Rocha is a senior analyst within the Peace and Security Programme at SaferAfrica where he is leading a process towards the development of minimum standards for the exploitation and management of natural resources in Africa. Rocha has a BA in human and social studies with specialisation in government, administration and development.

Notes

1 Chang Ning (2005) 'China's importation of mineral resources and oceanic shipping', *Chinascope*, June <www.chinascope.org>.

2 Energy Information Adminsitration <www.eia.doe.gov>.

3 Chietigj Bajpaee (2005) 'Sino-US energy competition', *Power and Interest News Report*, October.

4 Peter Brookes and Ji Hye Shin (2006) 'Chinese influence in Africa: implications for the United States', February.

5 Brookes and Ji (2006).

6 Brookes and Ji (2006).

7 Afrol News (2006) 'China, Angola sign 9 cooperation agreements', 7 March.

8 Princeton Lyman (2006) 'China's rising role in Africa', July.

9 Terradaily (2006) 'China given monopoly to work Gabon's untapped iron ore resources', 2 June.

10 According to Jörg Mayer and Pilar Fajarnes 'Tripling Africa's primary exports: What? How? Where?, during 1999–2003'.

11 Chinese Ministry of Commerce <www.mofcom.gov.ch>.

12 Afrol News (2006) 'China, Angola sign 9 cooperation agreements', 7 March.

13 Article 10 provides for public reporting of which measures should be put in place to allow access to information by members of the public in accordance with domestic law.

14 Article 1 (c) of the UN Convention against Corruption.

15 According to researchers like Raymond Baker and John Christiansen of the Tax Justice Network, the basic principle of mispricing entails: overpricing the goods that a country imports or underpricing the goods that it exports.

16 Selling goods or other components to local subsidiaries at inflated prices, which allows the companies to take profits through offshore accounts.

17 South Korea's Posco Engineering & Construction won an agreement that secures oil rights in exchange for building a 1,500km railway from Port Harcourt to Maiduguri (*Business Report,* 2006) 7 November <www.businessreport.co.za>.

18 The expression means that someone who has been hurt will be far more careful the next time.

19 An economic concept that links the exploitation of natural resources in a country with a decline in its manufacturing sector.

20 Illegal miners.

WHO'S AFRAID OF CHINA IN AFRICA? TOWARDS AN AFRICAN CIVIL SOCIETY PERSPECTIVE ON CHINA–AFRICA RELATIONS

NDUBISI OBIORAH

Economic, political and security cooperation between China and Africa has grown exponentially in the last decade, presenting new opportunities and challenges for Africa. The need for Africans to understand China, and its motives for the enhanced engagement with Africa over the last decade, is now greater than ever before, writes Ndubisi Obiorah.

An ever-closer embrace

Direct trade and political contacts between China and Africa date to the 15th century when an imperial fleet led by Admiral Zheng He visited East Africa in the course of a legendary global circumnavigatory expedition.[1] Indirect communication and trade between China and Africa, however, commenced over 3,000 years ago as evidenced by archaeological finds of Chinese ceramics in various parts of Africa as far apart as Timbuktu in West Africa's Sahel region to the Great Zimbabwe ruins and the Mozambique channel in southern Africa.[2]

The current form of China's engagement with Africa began taking shape after the 1949 revolution which brought Mao's Communist Party to power. From around 1950 to 1980 China assisted Africa's liberation movements and provided aid to over 800 projects in Africa, including initiatives in agriculture, fisheries, textiles, energy, infrastructure, water conservation and power generation.[3]

The 1980s heralded an end to Sino-African engagement based primarily on ideological or 'third world' solidarity, as Chinese development efforts were diverted inwards in tandem with policies enunciated by Deng Xiaoping. Through the 1990s, China increased its aid to African governments and resumed its earlier rhetoric of 'mutual respect' and 'concern for diversity' – a discourse that resounded strongly in a continent highly attuned to the perceived neocolonial reflexes of the former ruling powers. In return, Beijing received recognition of its sovereignty over Taiwan, indifference to its human-rights abuses, and support in international organisations from African countries.

In 2000, a new China-Africa cooperation forum agreed a joint economic and social programme. China has cancelled US$10 billion of the debt it is

---

Through the 1970s and 1980s,
the debate raged in Africa as to whether
Western political and economic models
could be transported to non-Western societies,
whether capitalism or Soviet-style socialism was
the better model for Africa or whether
African states could craft a
'Third Way' to nirvana.

---

owed by African states; at the second Sino-Africa business conference in December 2003, China offered further debt relief to 31 African countries, as well as opened the prospect of zero-tariff trade.[4]

Chinese trade and investment in Africa, particularly in terms of oil and natural resources, has increased rapidly as is apparent in Nigeria. During his April 2006 visit to Nigeria, President Hu and his Nigerian host, Olusegun Obasanjo, signed an agreement in which Nigeria would give China four oil drilling licences in exchange for a commitment to invest US$4 billion in infrastructure. The state-owned China National Petroleum Corporation (CNPC) received a right of first refusal on four oil exploration blocks at future auctions while China agreed to buy a controlling stake in Nigeria's 110,000 barrel-a-day Kaduna oil refinery and to build a power station. Other agreements signed at the time included a US$500 million export credit from the Eximbank of China to Nigeria, for infrastructure development, as well as a Chinese grant for anti-malaria drugs, to help train Nigerians to control malaria and bird flu and for cooperation in technology.

New horizons

The rapidly evolving relationship between China and Africa is reflected in the evolution of African perceptions of China and its motives for engagement with Africa. For decades during the cold war, the primary perception of China in much of Africa was as an ally against colonialism, neo-imperialism and Western domination, especially amongst left-wing circles. China was the alternate source to the Soviet Union of political, diplomatic and military assistance for African liberation movements. Post-liberation governments, however, often had to contend with Sino-Soviet rivalry for influence as well as the vexed question of Taiwan.

Chinese aid, particularly scholarships, was welcomed across Africa. In the eyes of many Africans, the Tan-Zam railway project established China's profile as a friend and ally against Western neocolonialism and the apartheid regime in South Africa. Chinese success in building a railway pooh-poohed by 'Africa hands' in the West was a turning point in Sino-African relations and led to wider recognition in Africa of China's growing industrial and technological prowess. Scholarships that enabled several thousand African students to access higher education in China also enhanced China's image as a friend of Africa.

From the 1950s, Chinese businesspeople from Hong Kong and Taiwan as well the overseas Chinese diaspora in south-east Asia established trading ties with African counterparts. Taiwan and Hong Kong were widely known across Africa by the early 1970s as sources for cheap imports of textiles and consumer goods although often of dubious quality. In particular, traders from south-eastern Nigeria established elaborate trade networks with

Hong Kong and Taiwan manufacturers and traders as well as with overseas Chinese businesses in south-east Asia.

From these initial trading contacts and visits, some Chinese businesses, especially manufacturers and traders from Hong Kong and Taiwan, began to establish representative offices and trading outposts in African countries in the late 1970s and eventually began to invest in manufacturing and trading operations in Africa. By the 1980s, there was a noticeable increase in Chinese residents and Chinese-owned businesses in many African countries. The introduction by the US government of preferential textile quotas for Africa

> *For many among Africa's ruled who are*
> *physically and intellectually exhausted by*
> *two decades of economic 'reform' supposedly*
> *adopted by African government but driven by*
> *Western governments, donors and the IFIs,*
> *China represents hope that another world*
> *is possible in which bread comes*
> *before the freedom to vote.*

encouraged some Chinese firms to establish operations in African countries to exploit this opportunity. The increased popularity of kung fu movies and the establishment of schools of martial arts in major African cities led to relatively greater awareness of China among ordinary Africans – although often with distorted perceptions of Chinese history and culture.[5]

Some Africans who visited China as students, traders or employees of Chinese businesses eventually stayed on and settled in China. In recent years, some Chinese companies, universities and schools have recruited employees (including academics and foreign language teachers) from the African diaspora in Europe and North America.[6] Reliable statistics on African residents in China are hard to come by for various reasons and since the late 1990s a considerable number of non-documented African migrants have settled in China. The growing number of African residents in China is widening and deepening people-to-people contacts between China and Africa and may soon attain some political significance.

Virtually in tandem with the shift in China's focus in its relations with Africa from ideology to trade, the dominant image of China in Africa by the 1990s had changed from ideological ally against colonialism, apartheid and Western domination to business partner and emerging economic colossus. The Chinese doctor or technical aid worker traded places with the Chinese entrepreneur or state corporation.

The impact on Africa of China's trade with Africa and the wider world as well as the activities of Chinese businesses operating in Africa elicits diverse perceptions from local populations and these deserve extensive and careful study as well as nuanced analysis. It is immensely difficult to attempt to describe popular perceptions in Africa of Chinese business or of China itself with a tolerable degree of accuracy because this is a relatively new area of scholarly inquiry and reliable information beyond anecdotal sources is hard to come by. Much of what appears in the African (and Western) media or the information provided by NGOs tends to be recycled, outdated, mono-dimensional – and sometimes little short of China-bashing.

Perceptions among Africa's political leadership and intelligentsia of the prospects and implications of China-African engagement warrant further research and measured analysis. China's offer of trade and aid without apparent political or humanitarian conditionalities is apparently much appreciated by some of Africa's politicians.[7] Approving China's investments in his country, Sahr Johnny, Sierra Leone's ambassador to Beijing, notes:

> We like Chinese investment because we have one meeting, we discuss what they want to do, and then they just do it. There are no bench-marks and preconditions, no environmental impact assessment.[8]

In much the same vein, China's provision to Zimbabwe of no-strings mili-tary assistance and economic cooperation following Western divestment, aid cancellation and pressure for change, led Emerson Mnangagwa, the speaker of Zimbabwe's parliament, to declare that 'With all-weather friends like the People's Republic of China … Zimbabwe will never walk alone.'[9]

Kenyan government spokesman, Alfred Mutua, describes China as 'an easy country to do business with' because:

> The Chinese do not peg their economic activity or aid to political conditions … you never hear the Chinese saying that they will not finish a project because the government has not done enough to tackle corruption. If they are going to build a road, then it will be built.[10]

It is noteworthy, however, that perceptions of China among Africa's political leaders go beyond appreciation for 'no-strings' aid and trade. China as an 'alternative' political and economic model to Western prescriptions appears to be a pervasive optic among African politicians, intellectuals, civil society and media. While the end of the cold war brought welcome changes including the end of proxy wars fought on Africa's soil and the liberation of Namibia and South Africa, the unipolar world characterised by the Western dominance that followed has been the source of much discomfort for many African intellectuals and political leaders.

In this light, China's emergence as a major axis of global power is often welcomed among African intellectuals, who hope that it may herald a return to global multi-polarity in which milieu Africa and the developing countries will have a greater role on the global stage than they currently do. The international relations scholar and former Nigerian foreign minister, Bolaji Akinyemi, welcomes 'strategic cooperation' between China and Nigeria. Noting that stronger ties between the Asian and African heavyweights were long overdue, he argues that:

> China is an emerging world power with a booming economy. She needs oil. Nigeria needs as much investment as possible, and to diversify the sources of its investment. In the Middle East, the United States regards China's incursion with alarm, but Nigeria is more virgin territory for suitors and Washington should not be too worried. It insulates Nigeria from influence by one power.[11]

China's breath-taking, state-led development reinvigorates African critics of the Washington consensus and encourages those who advocate that Africa look to East Asia for inspiration and political and economic models. The *Daily Trust* newspaper unfavourably compares Nigeria's economic policy management, particularly the adoption of economic reforms recommended by the World Bank and the International Monetary Fund (IMF), with China's economic policy. It calls for Nigeria's leadership to draw lessons from China's experience with economic reform. According to the paper:

In his celebrated book, *Globalisation and Its Discontents*, the winner of Nobel Prize in Economics, Joseph Stiglitz, showed that the miracle of China lies in good governance, public-private sector partnership and a genuine home-driven policy agenda as opposed to branded neo-liberal IMF/World Bank policies contained in the notorious Washington Consensus. China promotes the state-led gradualist reform agenda with remarkable social protection for the mass of potential losers as opposed to Nigeria's 'shock-therapy' reform in which a few winners are indulged while the mass of losers are left bare. China did not pursue a doctrinaire privatisation policy but encouraged state enterprises side by side [with] private enterprises with the eye on value-adding activities, employment-creation and inclusive development.'[12]

A Chinese model?

In a nuanced perspective on China, the senior leader of the Nigerian legislature, Senate President Ken Nnamani in a welcome address entitled 'China: A Partner and Example of Development and Democracy' during President Hu's April visit to Nigeria, describes China's 'outstanding (economic) performance exclusive of western democracy' as 'the paradox of development and democracy'. According to him:

China has become ... a good model for Nigeria in its quest for an authentic and stable development ideology ... China [is] a lesson to Nigeria on the enormous good that a focused and patriotic leadership can do to realise the dreams of prosperity and security for the citizens ... in embracing China ... it should not only be in [the] field of economic prosperity since ... [China's] steady and gradual democratisation confirms the lesson that no nation can sustain economic development in the long run without democracy.[13]

Nnamani's comments highlight the increasingly common perception in Africa of China as an alternate political and economic model to the Washington consensus. Since the mid-1980s, many African countries have been compelled to adopt a series of 'structural adjustment', 'economic recovery' and 'poverty reduction' programmes, often under pressure from Western donors and international financial institutions.

From the early 1990s, demands by Western donors that African governments adopt economic reforms prescribed by the World Bank and the IMF have often been bundled with so-called 'conditionalities' usually consisting of demands for 'political reforms' such as political liberalisation, the ending of one-party regimes, respect for human rights and so on. Environmental advocacy groups in Western countries often pressure their governments to demand environmental audits and impact assessments before funding new infrastructure and industrial projects in Africa.

When African post-colonial governments began moving towards one-party states and 'African socialism' in the 1960s, they often proffered the rationale that Western models of democracy were unsuited to Africa's material conditions and to its history and cultures. Through the 1970s and 1980s, the debate raged in Africa as to whether Western political and economic models could be transported to non-Western societies, whether capitalism or Soviet-style socialism was the better model for Africa or whether African states could craft a 'Third Way' to nirvana. The end of the Cold War and the apparent triumph of the Washington consensus led to a temporary cessation of the debate partly due to the disillusionment and intellectual exhaustion of the African Left.

When donor conditionalities were introduced, some African governments vigorously resisted the political conditionalities and argued that Western democracy was unsuited to Africa's needs and would fuel ethnic conflict and instability but their dissent was increasingly muted as aid flows dried up. Through the 1990s, it appeared that the debate had been settled for good and that most Africans, at least implicitly, accepted the thesis that political liberalisation and structural adjustment would lead to economic recovery in the short term and sustainable development in the long term. By the turn of the millennium, virtually no African government openly questioned the Washington consensus or suggested 'African alternatives'.

Many in Africa's civil society were and remain deeply conflicted over Western donor conditionalities and Western political and economic models. On the one hand, they actively welcomed political liberalisation in Africa and understood acutely that Western donor conditionalities were

> *Leading lights of the Obasanjo faction claimed that the absence of 'stability' and 'visionary leadership' were the principal cause of Africa's underdevelopment and that provision of the same by oligarchic ruling parties with long tenures in power had enabled Singapore and China to become contemporary economic miracles.*

often invaluable in securing the same. African NGOs often collaborated with Western NGOs to pressure Western governments to demand political liberalisation from African governments as a pre-condition for further development assistance.

On the other hand, many among Africa's intellectuals and civil society actors perceive the Bretton Woods-inspired economic reforms as having largely failed to alleviate or reduce poverty and, indeed, of having exacerbated poverty in Africa. They also note that many African governments have engaged in a political sleight of hand in adopting the absolute minimum in political reform such as to enable Western governments and aid bureaucracies to justify continuing aid flows to home legislatures, all the while vigorously resisting genuine democratisation.[14] African angst over the conditionalities is heightened by their external origins, which reinforce notions of powerlessness and irrelevance. Some African intellectuals perceive the world order since the end of the cold war as further marginalising Africa and reinforcing Western dominance.

China's emergence as a major economic power in the 1990s despite not being a democracy or adopting economic policies typically recommended by the international financial institutions (IFIs) has become a source of great interest for both Africa's rulers and ruled. For some among Africa's contemporary rulers, China is living proof of 'successful' alternatives to Western political and economic models. The semi-colonial Western domination of pre-revolutionary China is often cited as being analogous to Western colonialism in Africa in the early to mid-20th century while China's status as a developing country in the 1950s through the 1990s is also cited as coterminous with Africa's post-colonial experience.

For many among Africa's ruled who are physically and intellectually exhausted by two decades of economic 'reform' supposedly adopted by African governments but driven by Western governments, donors and the

> *The efforts of Africa's human rights advocates may be well served by projections that India may eventually surpass China's economic progress, thanks at least in part, to a freer political and intellectual culture.*

IFIs, China represents hope that another world is possible in which bread comes before the freedom to vote. Globalisation especially the phenomenon of 'jobless growth' has resulted in widespread popular disillusionment in Africa with structural adjustment and poverty reduction. This disillusionment creates conditions for debate as to the viability and efficacy of Western political and economic models in Africa.[15,16]

Given the democratic reversals experienced in much of Africa from the late 1990s onwards, there is a distinct possibility that some authoritarian regimes in Africa will seek to utilise China's economic success to rationalise avoiding further political liberalisation and genuine democratisation. Human rights advocates and democratic actors in Africa may increasingly find their traditional arguments, that respect for human rights and political liberalisation will inexorably lead to economic success, challenged by some African governments pointing to China as the poster-child for development sans democracy.

A mid-term prognosis could be some African governments invoking the 'China paradigm' to justify the adoption of state-led economic policies coupled with intensified political repression. Hu's April visit to Nigeria coincided with a long-festering political crisis sparked off by a major faction within the ruling Peoples' Democratic Party (PDP). The faction started trying to amend the constitution, in particular the prescribed term limits, so as to enable President Olusegun Obasanjo to remain in office for at least a further term of four years, and possibly for another three terms of four years each – in effect a life presidency given that General Obasanjo is widely believed to be in his mid-seventies.

Efforts by the Obasanjo faction to dominate the PDP through selective reregistration of party members and the disenfranchisement of members of rival factions within the ruling party led to serious regional and geopolitical fissures in Nigeria's politics. Among the principal justifications cited by proponents of the amendments were the economic success of modern China and Lee Kuan Yew's Singapore. Leading lights of the Obasanjo faction claimed that the absence of 'stability' and 'visionary leadership' were the principal cause of Africa's underdevelopment and that provision of the same by oligarchic ruling parties with long tenures in power had enabled Singapore and China to become contemporary economic miracles. Virtually harking back to the 'Asian values' and 'cultural relativism' debates on human rights and development in the early-mid 1990s, the proponents of this viewpoint argued that human rights and democracy are irrelevant to Africa's development needs, citing China as an exemplar of development sans democracy.

Virtually by stealth, the old debate about appropriate paths to Africa's development has been re-ignited by China's emergence as a major global power. The implications of this debate for advancing human rights and democracy in Africa are critical. A failure to re-establish the primacy and legitimacy of liberal democracy and strong human rights protections among Africa's intellectuals, media and civil society as the most appropriate path

45

for Africa's development may ultimately lead to popular disillusionment with Western-inspired political and economic prescriptions that are perceived as unable to put bread in the mouths of hungry infants while communist China becomes the workshop of the world. More important than the desires of some African governments to return to political illiberality is the danger of resurgence in the old, anti-Western, anti-democratic tendency among Africa's intellectuals, boosted by China's apparent success.

It is increasingly likely that a central challenge for civil society in Africa in the next few years will be an effort to prevent democratic reversal especially an 'intellectual rollback' to the 1970s. It may become necessary to re-establish or revalidate across Africa the legitimacy of democracy and human

---

Western commentators contend that China's lack of domestic political criticism frees its government and companies in their business endeavours in Africa from 'reputational risks' and other pressures that Western companies operating in Africa are routinely exposed to.

---

rights per se and also as the most appropriate and effective path to Africa's development. Africa's human rights advocates may be well served in this effort by projections that India may eventually surpass China's economic progress, thanks at least in part, to a freer political and intellectual culture. As the largest democracy in the world with long standing ties to Africa, India's economic progress in the last decade especially the exponential growth of its ICT industries could serve as an 'alternate' model to China.

There is encouraging evidence of nuanced perspectives among Africa's political leaders on China's rise without democracy. Nigerian Senate President Nnamani's comments above presage the realisation that the burgeoning Chinese middle classes will not accept indefinitely the prosperity-for-acquiescence offered by the Community Party and that China will in the long term evolve towards a representative form of government.

Furthermore, there is evidence of observers in Africa's media taking a not wholly uncritical assessment of China's progress and its implications for democracy and governance in Africa. An editorial in the Nigerian broadsheet *New Age* notes that 'The Chinese people have had to pay a heavy price in political repression and environmental degradation.'[17]

A human rights perspective

While China's rapidly expanding engagement in Africa is enthusiastically welcomed by African governments and some African intellectuals, China's relations with Africa's governments is often perceived among human rights NGOs and Western commentators as increasingly problematic for governance and human rights in Africa. China's increasing presence in Africa has generated a flurry of Western media reportage and commentary, often with graphic headlines, the prevailing note of which is that Chinese trade, political and security cooperation may enable repressive regimes in Africa to avoid even the relatively limited constraints on their conduct imposed by Western donor conditionalities. Elements in Africa's civil society are concerned about the potential implications of China's relationship with African governments for the advancement of human rights and democracy in Africa.

China–Africa security cooperation is particularly problematic. Chinese-made weapons are often cheaper than Western equivalents and China does not usually impose political, human rights or humanitarian conditions in its arms sales. The Nigerian government is increasingly turning to China for weapons to deal with the worsening insurgency in the oil-rich Niger Delta. The Nigerian air force purchased 12 Chinese-made versions of the upgraded Mig 21 jet fighter; the navy has ordered patrol boats to secure the swamps and creeks of the Niger Delta. Nigerian military officials have made clear that they will increasingly turn to China for weapons to quell the revolt in the Niger Delta which traditional Western suppliers appear reluctant to provide.

In particular, China's role in the Sudan crisis, where it has supported a military regime accused of perpetrating or at the very least encouraging ethnic cleansing has cast a disturbing light on Chinese engagement in Africa.[18] China bought 50 per cent of Sudan's oil exports in 2005, which presently accounts for 5 per cent of China's oil needs.[19] China is accused of blocking or diluting UN Security Council efforts to effectively address the Sudanese government's role in the humanitarian crisis in the Darfur region.

China's relationship with Zimbabwe also gives cause for concern. In return for providing the Mugabe regime with financial aid, machinery, equipment and military supplies, Chinese state-owned enterprises have made substantial investments in some of Zimbabwe's major national assets including hydroelectric power plants and tobacco production facilities. The Mugabe regime in Zimbabwe has made no secret of its turning to China for aid, military supplies and trade which Western governments will not provide. China supplied 12 fighter jets and 100 trucks to Zimbabwe's army even as the country is subject to a Western arms embargo.

Chinese assistance has enabled some African governments to embark on policies considered unwise by the IFIs and Western donors. Chinese loans in the last two years have enabled the Angolan government to embark on infrastructure projects regarded by the World Bank and the IMF as wasteful and unnecessary and to resist pressure from IFIs and NGOs for greater transparency and efficiency in the management of its oil revenues. Angolan oil accounts for 13 per cent of China's crude imports making China is the second-largest consumer of Angolan oil after the United States.

Human rights concerns about China's renewed engagement in Africa must of necessity extend beyond China–Africa intergovernmental relations. Indeed, it may be argued that in the near future, the role of the Chinese private sector in Africa may come to acquire as great a significance, if not greater, than that of the Chinese government or its state-owned enterprises in Africa. Some Chinese companies operating in Africa have been accused by NGOs of violating employment and environmental rights in the communities where they operate. NGOs in Nigeria have accused the Chinese logging company WEMPCO of discharging untreated effluents into the Cross River in south-eastern Nigeria, thereby damaging the health and livelihoods of local fisher folk. The company is also accused of colluding with local officials and law enforcement officers to suppress protests by the local community. The Chinese metalworking firm WAHUM, operating in Lagos, Nigeria, has also been accused by NGOs of discharging noxious substances into the air and systematic violations of occupational safety and health standards.

Western commentators contend that China's lack of domestic political criticism frees its government and companies in their business endeavours in Africa from 'reputational risks' and other pressures that Western companies operating in Africa are routinely exposed to. Whereas shareholders of Western companies may be cautious about investing in state-led energy projects in African countries which rely on a brutally-enforced stability, such issues have little visibility to the Chinese public.[20] This presents significant challenges for human rights advocates in Africa. Over the last two decades, transnational NGO networks and enhanced cooperation between African and Western NGOs have served to put pressure on Western governments and business in relation to human rights abuses and democratisation in Africa.

The ability of African human rights activists to call on colleagues in Western countries to mobilise pressure on their governments to, for example, demand that imprisoned opposition figures be released as a pre-condition for further aid flows, has served as an informal life assurance for many African activists. Given that many African governments are increasingly turning to China for political and economic cooperation, without the 'human rights and democracy strings' often imposed by Western governments, it seems likely that a significant source of leverage over their governments by African activists and their Western allies may be eroded.

A common African response?

An effective common African response at the governmental level appears unlikely for quite a while due to the structural weaknesses of Africa's regional organisation, the African Union. China effectively deals with Africa on its own terms via the China-Africa Cooperation Forum, which is convened by China. The AU, which should lead Africa's engagement with China, is enfeebled by the language and cultural divides which still plague Africa's regional politics.

A common African response is more likely at the civil society level where there is often a mutuality of concerns about human rights, democracy, labour and trade issues. Enhanced Africa-wide networking to develop common frameworks for responding to human rights and governance issues arising from China's role in Africa is imperative.

What can African civil society do?

Civil society in Africa is increasingly concerned with the role of China in Africa especially the Chinese government's relations with repressive regimes in Sudan and Zimbabwe. As China becomes a major weapons supplier to Africa's governments and Chinese energy and mining companies take up a substantial stake in resource extraction in Africa, these concerns can only grow.

China's enhanced presence in Africa is primarily driven by economic considerations; efforts to develop policy levers to prompt more constructive Chinese engagement in Africa will have to proceed from China's economic interests. Accordingly, African civil society cannot adopt the conventional 'naming-and-shaming' tactics that have served it well in addressing human rights abuses thus far; 'naming-and-shaming' tactics can, however, be adapted to deal with Chinese companies operating globally.

As a starting point, China studies in African universities and research institutions should be encouraged by African governments, private sector and civil society. In this respect, the pioneering introduction of Chinese language studies at the Nnamdi Azikiwe University in Nigeria and the University of Stellenbosch in South Africa are particularly noteworthy developments which should be replicated elsewhere in Africa.

African civil society should bring pressure through the African Union for a parallel civil society forum inclusive of business, labour and consumer groups to be instituted at the biennial meetings of the China-Africa Cooperation Forum. The parallel civil society forum would bring together non-governmental organisations from China and Africa to enhance people-to-people relations, exchange of ideas and perspectives and to lobby their respective governments to address the social dimension of China-Africa relations.

African civil society should take advantage of Western concerns about China's expanding role in Africa through 'coalitions of interest' with Western governments in raising concerns about governance and human rights in African countries where the Chinese government is deeply engaged with repressive regimes.

African NGOs can also work with Western NGO colleagues to mobilise threats of mass boycotts of Chinese-made consumer goods to protest

China's arms exports to repressive governments in Africa. To date, Chinese industry has distinguished itself primarily for cost-efficient manufacturing. As Chinese companies move up the global pecking order and discover the considerable mark-up to be derived from possessing premium brands and intellectual property, they will seek to establish their own brands rather than continue to serve as generic contract manufacturers or service providers to whom Western brands outsource production and support services.

As Chinese capitalism matures and global branding becomes more important to Chinese companies, they will be less willing to be associated

African civil society should seek to highlight to the Chinese government that its activities in Africa cannot be entirely risk-free in the absence of peace and stability, which cannot be secured in the absence of democracy and human rights.

with human rights abuses and repressive regimes in Africa and elsewhere. Chinese companies operating globally will thus become more vulnerable to 'naming-and-shaming' pressure from NGOs especially in Western consumer markets in relation to their image and associations.

The potential of violence directed at Chinese businesses and nationals in Africa by rebel movements who regard China as an ally of the local repressive regime is likely to compel China to re-examine its security cooperation with African governments. It may be argued that an 'all-comers-served' approach to security cooperation with African governments may not continue for much longer without significant cost to China.

Militant groups in the Niger Delta issued threats against Chinese interests and nationals following the signing of new oil and gas deals during President Hu's April 2006 visit to Nigeria. In an e-mail to news organisations, a spokesman for the militant group, the Movement for the Emancipation of the Niger Delta, (which has previously kidnapped Western oil workers and recently detonated two car bombs in the oil cities of Warri and Port Harcourt) criticised China for grabbing a US$2.2 billion stake in a Niger Delta oil field last year and stated:

> We wish to warn the Chinese government and its oil companies to steer well clear of the Niger Delta...Chinese citizens found in oil installations will be treated as thieves. The Chinese government by investing in stolen crude places its citizens in our line of fire.[21]

African civil society should seek to highlight to the Chinese government that its activities in Africa cannot be entirely risk-free in the absence of peace and stability, which cannot be secured in the absence of democracy and human rights. In particular, African NGOs can also highlight to the Chinese government that unrestrained exports of light arms exacerbate conflicts in Africa and worsen trafficking in small arms which may well end up being used against Chinese companies and nationals operating in Africa. In the Beijing Declaration issued at the first China-Africa Co-operation Forum in October 2000, the Chinese government committed itself along with African governments to strengthening their cooperation to stop the illegal production, circulation and trafficking of small arms and light weapons in Africa. African NGOs can and should take China up on this voluntarily accepted commitment.

While the Chinese government may not have to pay much regard to domestic public opinion, the Chinese government is historically very sensitive about its international image. China's abstention on a Security Council vote on Darfur in early 2006 should be cause for some guarded optimism. This suggests that China is not totally oblivious of potential harm to its global reputation if it came to be perceived as the principal patron and protector of Africa's tyrants. African NGOs can capitalise on this by coordinating actions and protests designed to embarrass the Chinese government at international forums such as international meetings and conferences, advocacy in local and global media institutions, contacts and interaction with senior Chinese officials and leaders. As the tempo of such sustained activity increases, the Chinese government will begin to reconsider its relations with countries where it has relatively marginal interests such as Zimbabwe. Such tactics may be less effective and may require a longer lead time against oil-rich countries such as Sudan.

After an initial phase of snapping up resource extraction concessions, it is almost conceivable that China will be compelled by instability and conflict in Africa to realise that its long term economic interests are best served by promoting peace in Africa and that this is most likely to come about by encouraging representative government in Africa rather than supporting dictators. As Chinese investors move beyond resource extraction to investments of a long-term nature, they will increasingly mount pressure on their government to avoid actions or policies likely to exacerbate instability or conflict.

In the long term, it is conceivable that greater internal political liberalisation within China will also result in less appetite for supporting repressive regimes in Africa.

Conclusion

The rapidly evolving China-Africa relationship offers immense opportunities for Africa but may also present new challenges. Africa should embrace the opportunities offered by strategic partnership with China, whilst seeking to preserve and promote its interests. By the nature of their trade, human rights NGOs and trade unionists tend to focus on the (potential) downsides of greater China-Africa engagement especially instances where repressive regimes have sought to avoid Western donor pressures for human rights, labour or environmental standards. Africa's civil society, however, needs to examine how best to react to the challenges presented by China's engagement in Africa and find a tolerable median between uncritical acceptance or knee-jerk rejectionism. In particular, Africa civil society can derive lessons from the experiences of other countries in engaging with China.[22]

The need for Africans to understand China and its motives for engagement with Africa is now greater than ever before. Relatively little is known about China among African civil society actors beyond Western media reportage. At a very minimum, they need to learn more about China as a country and its motives for engaging in Africa in order to develop a feasible agenda for responding to the opportunities and challenges presented by China's increasing engagement in Africa. However there is relatively little scholarly or policy literature on China-Africa relations generated within Africa. It is critical that civil society in Africa initiate efforts towards enhanced thought and action on the strategic implications of China's increasing engagement with Africa, particularly in relation to human rights and democracy in Africa.

Ndubisi Obiorah has been a visiting fellow and researcher at Harvard University, the National Endowment for Democracy and Human Rights Watch. He is currently director of the Centre for Law and Social Action (CLASA) in Lagos, Nigeria.

Notes

1 T. Luard (2005) 'China hails legacy of great adventurer', BBC News, 30 May <http://news. bbc.co.uk/2/hi/asia-pacific/4593717.stm> (accessed 25 May 2006).

2 C. Melville and O. Owen (2005) 'China and Africa: A New Era of "South-South Cooperation"', openDemocracy, 8 July <http://www.opendemocracy.net/globalization-G8/ south_2658.jsp> (accessed 25 May 2006).

3 M. Nduru (2004) *China and Africa in an Ever-Closer – Sometimes Thornier – Embrace.* Johannesburg: IPS <http://www.dehai.org/archives/dehai_news_archive/Nov04-Jan05/0465. html> (accessed 25 May 2006).

4 C. Melville and O. Owen (2005).

5 It is important to note that many ordinary Africans often have difficulty distinguishing nationals of the People's Republic of China from Hong Kong Chinese, Taiwan Chinese and overseas Chinese. From personal recollections of interaction with Chinese nationals in Nigeria in the early 1980s, it would appear that at least some Chinese residents were happy to maintain a strategic ambiguity.

6 Contacts between African immigrants in the West and China warrants further research. From anecdotal sources, an increasing number of African immigrants import 'Afro-centric' goods and materials such as textiles from Chinese 'contract' manufacturers for sale to African/Caribbean immigrant communities and to the African-American community.

7 H. French (2005) 'China Wages Classroom Struggle to Win Friends in Africa', *New York Times*, 20 November <http://www.howardwfrench.com/archives/2005/11/20/china_wages_ classroom_struggle_to_win_friends_in_africa/> (accessed 25 May 2006).

8 Lindsey Hilsum (2005) 'The Chinese are Coming', *New Statesman*, 4 July.

9 A. McLaughlin (2006) 'A Rising China Counters US Clout in Africa', *Christian Science Monitor*, 30 March <http://www.csmonitor.com/2005/0330/p01s01-woaf.html> (accessed 25 May 2006).

10 R. Crilly (2006) 'China Seeks Resources, Profits in Africa', *USA Today*
<http://www.usatoday.com/money/world/2005-06-21-africa-china-usat_x.htm> (accessed 25 May 2006).

11 Nigeria2Day (2006) 28 April.

12 *Daily Trust* (2006) 'The Widening Gap', 24 April.

13 C. Akunna, (2006) 'China Unfolds Five-Point Agenda for Africa', *THISDAY*, 28 April 2006
<http://allafrica.com/stories/200604280090.html>(accessed May 25 2006).

14 Notorious examples include Yoweri Museveni in Uganda, Meles Zenawi in Ethiopia, Lansana Conte in Guinea and Idriss Deby in Chad.

15 *Daily Trust* (2006).

16 Hu's April state visit sparked off fierce debate among Nigeria's chattering classes as to the utility of continuing with economic reforms prescribed by the IFIs and Western donors.

17 *New Age* (2006) 'Editorial', 31 March.

18 C. Alden (2005) 'Leveraging the Dragon: Toward "An Africa That Can Say No"', eAfrica, South Africa Institute of International Affairs, March <http://www.saiia.org.za/modules.php?op=modload&name=News&file=article&sid=513> (accessed 25 May 2006).

19 E. Pan (2006) 'China, Africa and Oil', Council for Foreign Relations, 12 January <http://www.cfr.org/publication/9557/> (accessed 25 May, 2006).

20 C. Melville and O. Owen (2005).

21 *Washington Post* (2006) 1 May.

22 S. Marks (2006) 'China in Africa – The New Imperialism?', *Pambazuka, News* 2 March
<http://www.pambazuka.org/en/category/features/32432> (accessed 25 May 2006).

AFRICA AND CHINA:
THEN AND NOW

KWESI KWAA PRAH TALKS TO
PATRICK BURNETT OF PAMBAZUKA NEWS

It is hypocritical of Western states to be concerned about how China is approaching Africa given their history of exploitative relations with Africa, says Kwesi Kwaa Prah. He also argues that it is futile for Africans to be pointing fingers at the West or at China. 'Africans have to organise their side of the story as best as they can in their own interests,' he says.

Pambazuka News: One of the articles in your forthcoming book deals with the earliest contact between China and Africa. Many people may not be familiar with that history. Could you explain it briefly?

Kwesi Kwaa Prah: It goes back to the early 15th century when the famous Chinese admiral Zheng made seven epic journeys to various parts of the world including Asia and Africa between 1405 and 1433. During the course of these journeys he visited Africa. This was about 80 years before Columbus so it goes very far back. It is even suggested that some of the maps that Columbus used he borrowed or had antecedence in Chinese global maps of that period.

Pambazuka News: And how did that history progress into China's relationship with Africa in terms of its engagement with newly independent African states of the 1950s and 1960s?

Kwesi Kwaa Prah: Well, there is a hiatus, an enormous hiatus, because of the distance and difficulty of communication and the colonial interlude which both China and Africa encountered. China went through a cycle which is not too different from the African cycle in terms of its encounter with the West and colonialism, from the period of the opium wars and the Boxer rebellion, the period of about a half century which ended in 1902-03. And then there was the period before China become a republic in 1912; and the era of the warlords, post 1912 to the beginnings of the Chinese revolution in the early 1920s; and then on from the early 1920s to 1948 when China, in the words of Mao Tse Tsung, 'stood up' in 1949.

Now after that China's contact with the rest of the world especially Africa and Asia started in earnest. By the time of the Bandung conference in 1955 China's beginnings of real contact with Africa was in the making and I'm talking about Africa proper, I'm talking about sub-Saharan Africa, non-Arab Africa and that is because China's relations with the Arab world were different and of an earlier period, but contact with Africa proper, black Africa, starts in earnest in the late 1950s and the rest is history.

Pambazuka News: So that's a period spanning several hundred years so the question then arises of how that influenced China's current approach to Africa and policy as outlined in the January policy paper released by the Chinese government.

Kwesi Kwaa Prah: Yes, well, you'll recall that there was a stage when Zhou Enlai, soon after or in the decade of African independence in the 1960s, visited East Africa and made the statement that Africa is 'ripe for revolution'. China supported the African liberation movements but was also in sharp rivalry with the Soviet Union. So the position China took was often not beyond consideration of its own tussles with the Soviet Union.

By and large China has been consistent in the sense that it has tried to help African states with infrastructure and at fairly low rates. This was particularly the case in the first two decades of independence before the Cultural Revolution in China itself. China did a lot to build roads and railways, to support African infrastructure and industrial plans, at a point in history when China itself was economically fairly weak.

Pambazuka News: Many have argued that the engagement with Africa in the 1950s and 1960s was more ideological, but that the current realities in an era of globalisation mean that China's interest in Africa is solely commercially driven.

Kwesi Kwaa Prah: I wouldn't put it in such polarised terms that at one end of the scale it is ideological and at the other it's all economic. I think what one can say is that it was preponderantly articulated and expressed in ideological terms in the earlier period. It also had economic dimensions but this was hardly pronounced. Now it is distinctly more pronounced as China tries to search for markets and also for raw materials.

Pambazuka News: So do you see that as a negative and positive engagement?

Kwesi Kwaa Prah: Well, I don't see it in positive or negative terms in the way that lots of people currently want to discuss the issues. China wants to pursue policies that are in its best interests and what we have to do in Africa is also to trade and pursue polices that are in our own interests. It's as simple as that – all states do that.

What I find a bit reprehensible is the tendency of certain Western voices to start making obstructionist [statements] or start raising concerns about China's attempt to get into the African market because it is a bit hypocritical for Western states to be concerned about how China is approaching Africa when they have had centuries of relations with Africa, starting with slavery and continuing to the present day with exploitation and cheating with subsidies which help the European Economic Community to ridiculous extents so that a cow in the European community gets a subsidy of $2 a day and 60 per cent of Africa doesn't get that. So we ask ourselves 'What is this concern? It is not real concern, it is jealousy and rivalry about Chinese inroads into Africa.

That is not to excuse the way China is approaching Africa. China is obviously also approaching Africa from its own interests or as it perceives its interests and some of this interest is not necessarily in the interests of Africa. This is something that Africa has to work out. It is futile for Africans to be pointing fingers whether at the West or at China. Africans have to organise their side of the story as best as they can in their own interests.

Pambazuka News: How should Africa go about doing that? What are some of the policy responses that are needed on the African continent?

Kwesi Kwaa Prah: Well, for a start I don't think Africa really has any chance of doing anything in this present world without unity. That is the bottom line. Africans have to unite. Africans divided as they are have no platform for bargaining with anybody. If Africa was united today it would be a world power, poor as it is, and it would be capable of dealing with China on its own terms or with the West on its own terms. Unity is the basic pre-requisite for African advancement and for Africa to be able to bargain with China or anybody else.

Pambazuka News: One of the articles in your book, authored by yourself, is entitled 'Nationalism, Revolution and Economic Transformation in China: Any Lessons for Africa?' What does China's example offer for Africa?

Kwesi Kwaa Prah: Well, you have to read my book first, that is for a start.

Pambazuka News: Can you give us a taster?

Kwesi Kwaa Prah: Well, I think one of the things we have to learn is that advancement in our time must be home grown. First, Africans have to learn to pull themselves up by themselves. Second, this process has to be based on their own cultural pre-requisites. It is not possible to develop Africa grounded in languages like English, French or Portuguese, or Arabic for that matter. Africans have to realise that the cultural base for development has to be their own. That is not to say they should not learn other languages, no, but they must make their languages the centre of all their development efforts.

Pambazuka News: China has cultural agreements with 42 African countries and 65 cultural exchange programmes in Africa. It has offered scholarships to 10,000 students and seconded more than 400 Chinese professors to African universities. Much of your work has been in the field of language and culture so what would you say are some of the issues raised by China's cultural involvement in Africa?

Kwesi Kwaa Prah: We still have to see a lot of this you know. These are projected plans, this is what they would want to do and it is very fresh. I don't think it has left the drawing board yet and I don't think the implementation is with us as of now. We will have to see how it pans out and how it is implemented. It is too early to make announcements about these plans.

Pambazuka News: When is the book due out and where can people get it from?

Kwesi Kwaa Prah: Well, I expect that the book will be out early in 2007. It should be available through the African Books Collective and bookshops in South Africa and also through the web. If you go to the Casas website [see below] you should be able to get the details.

Professor Kwesi Kwaa Prah is director of the Centre for Advanced Studies of African Society (Casas), which is based in Cape Town. Casas was established in 1997 as a Pan-African centre for creating research networks in Africa and its diaspora. Professor Kwaa Parah is the editor of a forthcoming book Afro-Chinese Relations: Past, Present and the Future. *Visit http://www.casas.co.za for more information.*

A podcast of this interview is available at http://www.pambazuka.org/en/broadcasts/podcasts.php.

TAKING OWNERSHIP
OR JUST CHANGING OWNERS?

ANABELA LEMOS AND DANIEL RIBEIRO

From the stripping of forest resources in Zambezia province to concerns about the effects a multi-billion dollar dam will have on surrounding communities, Anabela Lemos and Daniel Ribeiro ask whether, after a long history under Portuguese colonialism, Mozambique is not at risk of being colonised again under the flag of 'economic partnerships with China'. They write that concerns in Mozambique centre around China's weak social and environmental requirements, disregard for human rights protections, lack of transparency and policy of non-interference.

'Cahora Bassa is ours' are the first words Mozambique's president, Armando Guebuza, said after signing an agreement with Portugal's prime minister to transfer ownership of the 27-year-old hydropower dam on the Zambezi. The last link to Mozambique's colonisation by Portugal was finally broken, but are Mozambique's new economic ties following a similar pattern of exploitation and abuse?

Abusive economic interests are not something new in international relations, with extensive examples of the destabilising and crippling effects they can have on developing countries. These negative experiences have given foreign donors like the World Bank a bad reputation, and forced a number of donors to take social and environmental impacts more seriously and develop policies to address transparency, social justice and environmental sustainability. Past experience has shown that such protections are vital requirements in the quest for truly sustainable development.

However, one of the new overseas investors, the giant China, is rivalling the World Bank for honours as the biggest lender to African nations and undermining the lesson learnt of the importance of transparency, social jus-

> *one of the new overseas investors,*
> *the giant China, is undermining*
> *the lesson learnt of the importance*
> *of transparency, social justice and*
> *environmental sustainability*

tice and environmental sustainability. China's expanding demands for new energy and raw material (as well as markets for its own goods) has made Africa a focus point for obtaining these valuable natural resources and many of its nations are increasingly important economic partners. China is the biggest consumer of zinc, nickel, copper and crude oil and the top importer of tropical woods.

China's weak social and environmental requirements, disregard for human rights protections, lack of transparency and policy of non-interference in internal affairs of the countries they lend to has resulted in some African governments being shored up with funds while allowing them to avoid local and international pressure to clean up corruption. The result has been dictators maintaining power, centralising wealth, and avoiding true development.

Mozambique is one of the African countries that has latched onto China's funding approach and grabbed the opportunity of non-interference and weak policies with both hands. Below are some recent examples of the negative results of this relationship.

Logging in Zambezia province

Chinese timber buyers are colluding with Mozambican business people and some members of the Mozambique government and their forest services to strip precious slow-growing tropical hardwoods from Mozambique's semi-arid forests at a rate that could see the resource exhausted in 5-10 years, according to reports of the trade on timber and wood in the Zambezi. The unsustainable logging begins with Chinese support to timber buyers to acquire 'simple licences', which allow logging of a relatively small quantity in a specific area. These licences are given to local Mozambicans, in large numbers (146 in 2003 alone), thus starting a deforestation process often referred to as 'the Chinese takeaway'.

Once an application has been approved, the licence holder pays for the licence (US$10–40 per cubic meter of forest logged depending on the species). Many of the local licence holders get credit from Chinese buyers to pay these expenses. The availability of this credit is the main factor driving the logging boom, attracting unqualified and unskilled people into the sector. Up to one-third of operators do not repay their debts, and this cost is passed on to other operators, in lower prices paid for the timber. On average the income generated by locals linked to the logging industry is below the legal minimum wage of US$30/month.

The quotas and licences give little indication of the quantity and area of logging; under-reporting is systematic and widespread. Inspections are rare, bribes common, and the computer-based control system of licensing and

---

starting a deforestation process
often referred to as
'the Chinese takeaway'

---

transport is purely cosmetic, according to reports and local experts. There is only one real checkpoint at Nicoadala, where copies of all the licences of all the operators are filed and where all drivers should stop. Anyone looking into the matter who spends time at the checkpoint will notice that the focus is on villagers with small volumes of hand-sawn timber and established industrial operators, while operators well connected to politicians, the Provincial Forests and Wildlife Services of Zambezia (SPFFB) and the timber buyers are allowed to escape. In 2002, the quota was set at 42,000m^3 (1,132,000ha total area of concessions) but SPFFB reported only 33,200m^3 (+/- 97,600 logs), of which only 28,400 m^3 (+/- 83,500 logs) was exported. However, that year 17 bulk carriers and 27 container ships loaded logs in the port, totalling 51,000m^3 (+/- 150,000 logs) based on the port authorities' record (also believed to be an underestimate by local experts).

For example in late October 2004, the bulk carrier *Chang Ping* docked in the port of Quelimane to load 2,000–2,500 tons of logs, according to the head of the company owning the ship. The local exporter (Madeiras Alman), however, officially declared a total weight of only 1,074 tons (4,715 logs with a total volume of 1,602m³). The ship was in port loading for 10 days into three holds simultaneously for 24 hours per day. Even with slow manual loading, at a rate of 20 logs per hour, and accounting for work stoppages, approximately 10,000 logs could have been loaded.

The manipulation does not stop with the statistics and data, but also involves the regulations. Originally, the main commercial species (Class 1) had to be processed prior to export. However, just as the regulations were coming into force, the ministry, under pressure from the logging industry, passed a special regulation (or 'ministerial diploma'), reclassifying the commercial timbers to permit their export as logs. Now the unprocessed logs are exported to China, undermining local industry and transferring most of the benefits from one of the poorest countries in the world to what is becoming one of the richest. What is happening in Zambezia Province is replicated or even worse in other provinces such as Cabo Delgado, Nampula and Niassa. Rather than combating illegal logging, China, through measures including the manipulation of forest regulations, false technical information and statistics, bribes and indirect involvement in logging, is actually facilitating illegal logging and hindering sustainable development in the sector.

Mpanda Nkuwa dam

The proposed Mphanda Nkuwa dam is a good example of the problems linked to China's lack of concern for human rights and the environmental impact of the projects they are financing. The US$2.3 billion Mphanda Nkuwa dam proposal has caused considerable debate in Mozambique with civil society and the potentially affected communities raising numerous concerns. The project's weak social and environmental assessment, high economic, environmental, social and technical risks and many other negative impacts, have put Western funders such as the World Bank off the project. In spite of these problems, early this year the China Ex-Im bank, China's overseas lending arm, agreed to back the construction of the dam project.

The Mphanda Nkuwa dam will have a capacity of 1,350 megawatts and will be on one of Africa's most dammed rivers, the Zambezi. The dam's electricity will be directed primarily towards industry and southern Africa's regional grid, completely ignoring the fact that less than 5 per cent of Mozambican's have access to electricity. The production of the power will cause twice daily fluctuations in the river's flow, which will adversely affect the people downstream that depend on the river for suitable and acceptable access to water, fishing, river navigation and flood recession farming.

The dam will also undermine years of restoration work in the Zambezi delta (East Africa's richest wetland and a Ramsar 'wetland of international importance' site), which has been damaged by the mismanagement of the

> *The quotas and licences*
> *give little indication of the quantity*
> *and area of logging; under-reporting*
> *is systematic and widespread.*

Cahora Bassa dam, just over 70km upstream of Mphanda Nkuwa. A daily flow regime and flood simulation is being suggested for Cahora Bassa dam to better support downstream ecology and meet environmental flow requirements. However, the Mphanda Nkuwa dam flow regime has been based on Cahora Bassa's present destructive one, and the project environmental impact assessment states that if that is changed it could make Mphanda Nkuwa uneconomic. It is likely, therefore, that the years of work to begin restoring the Zambezi downstream of Cahora Bassa will be dropped in favour of getting more hydroelectricity out of the river.

The recent 7.5 earthquake and several aftershocks in Mozambique have justified already existing concerns about the seismic risk linked to the Mphanda Nkuwa project. The country is in the vicinity of the Nubia-Somalia plate boundary and straddles a highly active fault zone called the Shire trough, which runs southward from the southern point of Malawi almost all the way to Maputo. Thus the country is considered to be in a seismically active zone, but poor records in the area severely constrain scientists' ability to determine the potential for large earthquakes. For example, the recent 7.5 earthquake was nearly 13 times bigger than had been thought possible along that fault.

The Mphanda Nkuwa dam will be in this seismically active area, just 200km from the heart of the Shire trough fault zone. In addition, the shape of the Shire trough means that the dam's reservoir could increase the surrounding plates' seismic potential as a result of the increased weight of the water – a phenomenon known as 'reservoir-induced seismicity' or RIS.

It is likely, therefore, that the years of work to begin restoring the Zambezi downstream of Cahora Bassa will be dropped in favour of getting more hydroelectricity out of the river.

Furthermore, the Estima fault crosses the reservoir 25 metres from the proposed dam wall. It is thought that this fault is active despite there being no activity in the recent geologic record. Mozambique's lack of experience with and knowledge of large dams and China's low social and environmental requirements, coupled with the weak data available for the area, increases the risk and creates the potential for a major disaster.

The China Ex-Im Bank's funding is intended to promote the export of Chinese mechanical and electronic products and high- and new-tech products, to support Chinese companies with comparative advantages, to 'go global' with offshore construction contracts and overseas investment projects. The bank's involvement in Mphanda Nkuwa has removed the pressure on the Mozambique government to improve the social and environmental assessments of this project and has enabled the government to avoid addressing its various negative impacts. If the Mphanda Nkuwa dam project goes ahead in its present form, it will be another example of the negative impacts of large dams and will significantly handicap Mozambique's development.

Other dam projects in Africa have not set an encouraging precedent. There have been serious human rights abuses around the Merowe dam in Sudan, for example (see the article by Ali Askouri). Its resettlement programme has been very poor, there has been no transparency, and it has a bad record on environmental and social assessment. Closer to home, in Zambia, state utility ZESCO is working with the Chinese company Sinohydro on the Lower Kafue gorge project. It chose a dam site after a balanced assessment of the economic, social and environment factors. However, we have learned from an inside source that Sinohydro told ZESCO that it was not how they did things in China and that they wanted to see a site assessment that focused only on economic factors. In the end, the original ZESCO site was selected, but the role of the Chinese dam builders in trying to focus only on the economics of the project does not bode well.

We also hear allegations from the coastal fishing communities of illegal fishing from Chinese boats, using longliners and gill nets that not only capture turtles and sharks but are also destroying our coastal zone. It was reported that in October 2005 a Chinese ship docked in Maputo harbour with around 4 tons of illegal shark fins. No information was available on the species of the sharks, where they were caught or the method used. The Chinese illegal fishing boats are taking advantage of our government's lack of interest in or means to control and monitor our coastal area, and are destroying it and the livelihoods of the local communities.

The economic link with China is still a young and growing partnership with numerous investments in the pipeline. The few current investments have shown a tendency towards exploitation and abuse. The secrecy of the negotiations, whether it is Cahora Bassa or Mphanda Nkuwa, the conditions of the funding and the disregard of the basic building blocks of development such as equality, social justice, a healthy environment and equity make us wonder if we Mozambicans are taking ownership of our country or just changing owners. What are the costs to our people and land? What will be the heritage of future generations? What is ahead of us? After so many years of being colonised by the Portuguese, are we now being colonised again, in the name of development but under the new flag of 'economic partnerships with China'?

Anabela A.Lemos is a Mozambican environmental activist and founder member and director of JA! (Justiça Ambiental).
Daniel L.Ribeiro is a Mozambican biologist, researcher and environmental

activist. He is a founder member of JA! (Justiça Ambiental) and coordinator of the Water Rivers and Development unit in JA!

Bibliography

R.D. Beilfuss and B.R. Davies (1998) 'Prescribed flooding and wetland rehabilitation in the Zambezi Delta, Mozambique', in W. Streever (ed.) International Perspectives on Wetland Rehabilitation. Dordrecht: Kluwer

Justiça Ambiental (2003) 'How does Mphanda Nkuwa comply with the World Commission on Dams?', funded and prepared for IRN

Justiça Ambiental (2003–06) Zambezi trip reports and interviews from various projects

Catherine Mackenzie (2006) 'Forest governance in Zambezi, Mozambique – Chinese takeaway – Final report for FONGZA'

D. Ribeiro (2005) 'The Zambezi Valley damned by dams'

UTIP (2002) 'Mphanda Nkuwa projects data summary' <http://www.utip.org.mz/pf/>

UTIP (2002) 'Mphanda Nkuwa and Cahora Bassa North feasibility study', environmental impact assessment, World Bank site

CHINA'S INVESTMENT IN SUDAN: DISPLACING VILLAGES AND DESTROYING COMMUNITIES

ALI ASKOURI

Ali Askouri charts the high cost of China's rising involvement in Sudan, placing emphasis on the lives lost and communities displaced in the Southern Sudan and Darfur. He explains the rapidly growing Chinese demand for oil and the involvement of Chinese companies in huge infrastructure projects. 'The sad truth is, both the Chinese and their elite partners in the Sudan government want to conceal some terrible facts about their partnership,' writes Askouri. 'They are joining hands to uproot poor people, expropriate their land and appropriate their naturaul resources.'

Before Sudan's independence in 1956, the nation's economic relations with China were insignificant. Despite good diplomatic relations, the level of cooperation between the two countries hardly figured on Sudan's foreign-trade sheet. From independence up to the early 1990s, Sudan exported cotton, sesame, and metal scraps to China. In exchange, Sudan received small arms, fabrics and other textiles. At one point, however, in the early 1970s, the Chinese built what they called the 'Friendship Hall' – a grand conference hall on the Blue Nile's western bank, a few hundred metres from the confluence of the White and Blue Niles at Khartoum. Available data showed that Sudan's total debts to China up to 2001 totalled US$67.3 million, of which China wrote off 63 per cent[1] in 2001. *WRITING OFF DEBT*

In 1989, however, there was a military coup in Sudan. Led by Islamic officers and widely supported by the National Islamic Front, the junta declared a holy war on the Southern Sudanese rebels who were fighting the central government at the time. The main objectives of the coup were:

71

- To crush the rebels
- Islamicise and Arabise the southern part of the country
- Forcibly unite the South with the rest of the country
- Establish an Islamic state.

To achieve its objectives the junta set out to exploit the country's vast oil reserves, discovered by Chevron in 1978. The country was opened up for Islamist investment and many Islamic groups came to the country with huge amounts of money. However, it soon became apparent that these groups lacked the necessary technical expertise required for such ventures. Consequently, not long after they had settled, the junta expelled them under various political pretexts.[2]

As a result of a trade and financial boycott by the donor community and international financial institutions,[3] Sudan was facing bankruptcy. To overcome these economic difficulties, the junta began feverishly looking for an influential business partner who could extract oil and mobilise other natural resources to lubricate its atrophying economic muscles. Given its recent human rights records, the human and material costs of any investment were never issues that the junta was going to care about. Indeed, the junta had shown exceptional cruelty towards the civil and political rights of citizens, even those who did not antagonise the junta. It was therefore expected that violations of rights would become excessive when civil and political rights collided with the junta's declared agenda.[4]

Following its experience with the Islamists groups, the junta wanted its business partner to have the strength and ability to withstand political pressure from Western 'imperialist' countries; the stamina and determination not to be bothered by the protests of human rights groups; and, above all, to be a heavyweight international player that Western imperialist countries would find hard to force out of the country through political pressure.

China's long-term strategy for Africa

Numerous events in different African countries since the beginning of the 21st century have show that there is a long-term Chinese strategy to control and exploit Africa natural resources, particularly oil. The Chinese strategy is propelled by China's growing internal demand for oil as a result of its rapid economic growth. The key African countries targeted by the strategy include, but are not limited to, Sudan, Ethiopia, Angola, Chad, Algeria, Equatorial Guinea, Gabon, Nigeria, Zimbabwe, Mozambique and Ghana. Although the current economic development status of these countries cries out for development targeted at improving the lot of the impoverished masses, this is not the motivation of Chinese economic assistance. Following a top-down economic development approach, Chinese economic assistance to these African countries has encouraged elitism, deepened social and class divisions and widened corruption.[5] Economic assistance seems targeted to

NEGATIVE IMPACT

> *To overcome these economic difficulties,*
> *the junta began feverishly looking for*
> *an influential business partner*
> *who could extract oil and mobilise*
> *other natural resources to lubricate its*
> *atrophying economic muscles.*

reward or bolster whomever is in power, regardless of how they got there. While many African societies struggle to further democratic values and strengthen respect for human rights, there is no doubt that Chinese economic assistance is encouraging dictatorships and tyranny in Sudan, Chad, Zimbabwe and elsewhere.

Chinese leaders keep repeating the misleading statement that China does not interfere in the internal affairs of the countries it deals with. This statement is untrue, provocative and insulting to many Africans who are aspiring to further democratic values. China interferes deeply in the domestic affairs of its partners, but always to the benefit of the ruling group. A recent meeting between the Sudanese president and his Chinese counterpart revealed the extent of China interference in domestic Sudanese affairs in favour of the ruling junta. Addressing his Chinese counterpart, the Sudanese president stated: 'The relationship with China has been fraternal, brotherly and excel-

[handwritten at top: China has interfered in Sudan through its politic[al] support and financing (especially arms), furthermore, it blocked UN sanctions & embargoes and it has placed high levels of Chinese UN troops.]

lent. Our relation with China is built on mutual benefit. China has always supported the unity of Sudan. When our relations became problematic with the international financial institutions, we turned to China. Relations with China have enabled us to overcome economic difficulties.' The Chinese president has expressed support for the Sudanese president's concerns about United Nation troops being sent to the Darfur region: 'China is sympathetic to Bashir's objections against peace-keeping forces'.[6]

In Sudan, Chinese support for the government has undoubtedly undermined all the efforts of the opposition to effect change in the government, thereby extending its rule despite the clear political indications that the junta would be unable to rule the country without heavy Chinese economic and military support.[7] It is therefore not surprising that Chinese economic aid to the Sudanese junta has come at an extremely high human cost in Southern Sudan and Darfur, where the number of lives lost and communities displaced has become an internationally recognised tragedy.

[handwritten in margin: DEPENDENCY THEORY]

History of China-Sudan relations

As early as 1992–94, hundreds of Chinese, allegedly employed by Chinese intelligence, started to appear on Khartoum streets selling cheap consumer products directly to the people. Some of these people became involved in house construction while others set up small commercial companies. The tens of thousands of Chinese workers who were later recruited for the construction of the oil pipeline and other mega-infrastructure projects were gradually moved into Sudan this way.[8] In those days the phenomenon of hundreds upon hundreds of young Chinese (mostly men in their 20s) who neither speak Arabic nor English, crowding the dusty streets of Khartoum selling combs and headscarves to people was the talk of the city. Apparently it was hard for the local people to understand how a young chap could fly in from Shanghai to sell combs and deodorants on Khartoum's streets in order to make a living!

Inside China, the rapidly growing demand for oil pushed China to venture into Africa looking for opportunities. 'The reality that China faces is that it will need to become a net importer of oil by the year 2000 if it is going to continue with its modernisation plans,' wrote Cleophas Lado of the University of the Western Cape.[9]

Indeed, endowed with its vast recoverable oil reserves, Sudan was a great opportunity for China. Equally, for the Sudanese junta, China – given its exceptional ability to condone human rights abuses alongside its heavy-weight ability to develop large-scale projects – represented the ideal partner with whom to strike a deal. 'It is very much a symbiotic relationship between China and Sudan, where China is in desperate need of a secure source of oil over the long term, while Sudan needs the external credit, investment and market for its oil.'[10]

Lado describes a few of China's investments in Sudan: 'China has invested heavily in the country. China has initiated $20 billion worth of development and infrastructure projects involving dams, hydroelectric power

While many African societies struggle to further democratic values and strengthen respect for human rights, there is no doubt that Chinese economic assistance is encouraging dictatorships and tyranny in Sudan, Chad, Zimbabwe and elsewhere.

stations, textile mills and agricultural schemes. China has promised to contribute $750 million in the construction of the new Khartoum international airport, and another $750 million for a new dam on the Nile in the Northern Province. Approximately $100 million has been spent by the Chinese on textile plants, and $500 million on a recently constructed oil refinery. China also provided Sudan with over $12 million in soft loans to fund a fishing project in the Red Sea. Other economic ties have involved arms transfers between Beijing and Khartoum. China has supplied the Khartoum government with arms since 1985, with transfers between 1985 and 1989 totalling $50 million. China became one of the GOS's [government of Sudan's] principal arms suppliers in 1994 and remains so today. China is a preferred supplier in that it attaches no conditions to its arms sales other than monetary ones and oil concessions, and its weapons are relatively cheap. China sold Sudan SCUD

missiles in 1996 in a deal underwritten by a $200 million Malaysian govern-
ment loan against future oil extraction. In 1990, the GOS signed a deal worth
$400 million whereby China would supply arms to Sudan and receive cot-
ton in return.'[11]

In addition to Lado's list of Chinese projects in Sudan, China is upgrad-
ing the Khartoum oil refinery from 50,000 barrels/day (b/d) to 70,000 b/d
at a cost of US$350 million.[12] As part of the Merowe dam project (also being
built by the Chinese, see below), the Chinese won a second contract for

---

*China interferes deeply in
the domestic affairs of its partners,
but always to the benefit of
the ruling group.*

---

power towers that will transport electricity from the dam site to Khartoum
and Port Sudan. The contract signed by Harpin-Jilin and CCMD is worth
about US$460 million.[13] This is in addition to a bridge project downriver
from the dam site costing US$10 million. Chinese companies are also build-
ing pump stations on the riverbanks for resettlement projects for the dam-
affected people. The cost of these projects was not made public.

Chinese companies are also building another two bridges on the main
stream of the River Nile in northern Sudan at Al Matamha and Al Damr.
The cost details have not been made public. The Chinese Boli company[14]
will build another two bridges, one on the Blue Nile between Al Hasahiesa
and Rufa'a, the other on the White Nile at Al Diwaim. The cost of the two
bridges is US$30 million.[15] The Chinese CMIC received a contract for US$373
million to build a pipeline to transport water from near the confluence of
the Atbara River with the main Nile to Port Sudan. The same company has
another contract for US$5.2 million for the water supply in Atbara and Al
Damr.[16] According to the *Al Ray Al A'am Daily*, an unnamed Chinese company will build the fourth Gaurri power station to produce 100MW of electricity. The value of the contract is not given.[17] Another contract was signed
with the Chinese company Harpin to upgrade the Gaurri (2) power station

from 120MW to 240 MW. The contract amount is not stated.[18] In addition to these, CMSC is building the Rabak silo with storage capacity for 100,000 metric tonnes of cereals. The contract is worth US$722 million, according to the paper.[19] Another Chinese company has also won a contract for deepening the Port Sudan seaport. Chinese Engineering Works co-signed a contract with the Sudanese Ministry of Transport amounting to US$79 million.[20]

While China claims that it does not interfere in internal politics, the distribution of these projects reveals that China is immersed in the internal politics of Sudan up to its neck. However, Chinese immersion in internal politics is meant to appease the ruling elite, with minimal analysis of the economic, social and environmental feasibility of the proposed projects. For China, whoever happens to be in power is a friend of China as long as they will guarantee China access to resources. Indeed, the opportunistic nature of Chinese policy in Africa is very obvious. It has led, as discussed below, to massive internal displacement and is associated with the loss of hundreds of thousands of lives – tantamount to genocide in many parts of Sudan.

Chinese investment in Sudan is linked to massive population displacement and, according to the US Congress, genocide in the western Sudan region of Darfur.[21] Here we discuss two major projects in which China is involved: oil extraction and the Merowe dam in Northern Sudan.

Displacement and human rights abuses in oil producing areas

Currently most of Sudan's oil is produced in the Upper Nile area. The Dinka and Nuer people are the main tribes living in the area. To ensure the safety of the oil installations, the government adopted a scorched-earth policy carried out by the army and splinter groups from the Sudan Peoples' Liberation Movement, used by the government as proxies to carry out its depopulation policy of the area. According to Christian Aid:

> The inter-tribal warfare that has plagued the south for the last decade has been fomented by strategic arms deliveries from government garrisons. By the middle of last year, hundreds of cases of ammunition

had already been delivered to one of the southern factions fighting for control of Western Upper Nile and its vast oil reserves. This is warlordism – as the government and the oil companies call it – but warlordism provoked and encouraged by the government with the express intent of depopulating oil-rich areas.[22]

The policy was carried out with an intensity that leaves no doubt that the inhabitants must leave or face death and extermination. The report continues:

Since construction of the pipeline to the Red Sea began in 1998, hundreds of thousands of villagers have been terrorised into leaving their homes in Upper Nile. Tens of thousands of homes across Western Upper Nile and Eastern Upper Nile have been burnt to the ground. In some areas, the charred remains of the humble mud huts that got in the way of oil are the only evidence there is that there was ever life in the region.[23]

As mentioned earlier, China's involvement in Sudan goes beyond oil. Indeed, in all the other projects the behaviour of Chinese companies has been identical to that in the oil sector. The dam project currently being implemented by Chinese companies on the River Nile has sad similarities – in terms of cost and displacement – to the oil project.

Displacement in the Merowe dam project

The Merowe dam (also known as the Hamdab dam) is a massive multipurpose dam project on the fourth cataract of the River Nile in Northern Sudan. The dam, which is expected to cost around US$1.8 billion,[24] is being implemented by a Chinese joint venture between China National Water Resources and Hydropower Engineering and China Water Engineering, known as CCMDJV, according to the dam implementation unit website[25] and other Sudanese and European companies. The CCMDJV contract totalled US$60 million.[26] Chinese companies have another contract in the project for power tower networks that extend to Dongola, Atabara, Portsuan and Khartoum. The total amount of the Chinese contract is US$460 million. The project, according to the dam authority, will displace more than 50,000 small farmers living on the riverbanks.

As in the oil sector, clearance of landowners on and near the dam site followed. On 13 December 2003, the website Sudaneseonline reported:

On Sept. 30th, a group of men, women and children of Korgheli Village demonstrated against the dam around the dam site. The police ruthlessly attacked them using live bullets, tear gas and plastic rods. Three men were shot, severely injured and were taken to Karima Hospital. A number of women were injured in the scuffles with the police. Colonel (Retired) Altayeb Mohammed Altayeb (President of the union of the affected people) and Mr. Abdel Mutalab Tai Allha (Union deputy President) were both arrested on site and taken to Kober prison where they were detained for a month and were subjected to torture and abuse.

On Dec. 1, the police again attacked the people of Korgheli village who refused to move and opted to stay in the ruins of their village houses, which had been destroyed by the dam contractors. The police attacked them dispersing them and eventually closed down the primary school and the health centre to force them to move from their demolished houses.[29]

However, as in most dam projects these poor villagers were forcibly resettled in a desert location by the dam authority.

In February–March 2005, two leading experts on dams and resettlement visited the site and reported:

Al Multaga site is located in the desert. The Merowe Dam Project Implementation Unit (MDPIU) is providing support in removing the sand that covers many plots and in irrigating the land. However, two years after resettlement, some 20% of the land has still not been cleared of sand; it is thus unavailable for production. And even with irrigation, the quality of the soil is so poor that farmers cannot sell their products on the market.[30]

> *not only do the Chinese companies not respect*
> *human rights in their investments, they rely on*
> *armed forces and security personnel to enable*
> *them continue their appropriation of natural*
> *resources at the expense of poor people*

The shootings and detention of the Hamdab people sent shocks around the communities affected by the dam project. The two other groups felt they would also suffer the fate of the Hamdab. Preparing themselves for the worst, the communities formed an armed movement (Movement of the Displaced, or MOD)[31] to defend their land.[32] Once MOD declared itself, the security started a witchhunt among the leaders of the communities.[33] This, however, was only the beginning of their nightmare. In November 2005, the Chinese contractors building the power tower network occupied water wells in the Bayuda deserts and prevented the Manasir nomads from accessing the water.[34] The nomads reported the incident to the committee of the affected people, which in response decided to hold a meeting in the area to show solidarity and support for the nomads. The Chinese, who carry out their work in close coordination with security organs and the armed forces, called on them for protection. The people who flocked to the meeting in their thousands were shocked to discover that their peaceful gathering was surrounded by heavily armed army units. A journalist who covered the meeting said that 'bloodshed was hardly avoided'.[35]

Indeed, these events and the growing tension between the Chinese contractors and the government on the one side and the affected people on the other did not prompt the Chinese to re-examine their involvement in the project. On the contrary, events that followed showed that not only do the Chinese companies not respect human rights in their investments, they rely on armed forces and security personnel to enable them continue their appropriation of natural resources at the expense of poor people.

On 22 April 2006 the dam militia, armed with machine guns and heavy artillery, attacked Amri people who were meeting in the local school courtyard to discuss how to organise themselves against the dam authority's plan to forcibly displace them to the desert. The attacking militia opened fire on the people without warning, killing three on the spot and injuring more than 50.[36] However, despite condemnation from all political forces and human rights groups,[37] the Chinese manager of the project, **Ding Zhengguo**, the vice-president of China International Water and Electrical Corp, in a reply to the Business and Human Rights Resource Centre completely **denied the incident had taken place**.[38] However, Mr Ding confessed a terrible truth that China's officials have long denied. For many years China's officials have refused to admit that their investments in certain African nations depend on the ability of the ruling elite to protect their personnel, through excessive state power if necessary. As Mr Ding states:

> Please be informed that the government of Sudan has assigned local security force to be responsible for the security of Merowe dam project at both upstream site and downstream site of the project construction area. Security personnel from professional security companies engaged by contractors and approved by the client and engineer are also 24 hours available for the security of the site camp and construction site.[39]

In Sudan, it has been the established tradition that major public infrastructure projects are normally guarded by the police force or in exceptional cases by small army units. Staff working on such projects normally live among local people without any type of protection. On the assumption that the Chinese are investing their money to help poor Sudanese, it is odd that they believe the dam site should need security protection 24 hours a day. It is even more puzzling given that in that part of Sudan – where villagers are all connected or related to each other – theft or crime of any sort are unheard of. Villagers still leave their doors unlocked. From what, then, do the Chinese need protection?

The sad truth is, both the Chinese and their elite partners in the Sudan government want to conceal some terrible facts about their partnership. They are joining hands to uproot poor people, expropriate their land and appropriate their natural resources.

Conclusion

Commenting on China's foreign policy, Lado states

> From Sudanese experience it looks that the strategy of China's foreign
> policy is not built on initiative and entrepreneurship, it rather exploits
> the opportunities resulting from the contradictions in the international
> arena. For China Sudan was the best opportunity that China could
> dream of given its rising domestic demand for fuel and the growing
> internal trend among Chinese investors for overseas investment.[40]

The opportunistic nature of Chinese foreign investment, particularly in
Sudan, was further exposed when pressures mounted on the Sudanese
government to accept peacekeeping forces in Sudan. China failed to veto
any United Nation Security Council Resolutions on Darfur, including the
referral of Darfur criminals to the International Criminal Court. This has
led many Sudanese commentators to question the feasibility of maintaining
a strong link with China and whether China is a trustworthy and reliable
political ally.

One reason China is the single biggest international player in Sudan
is the prolonged boycott by Western countries of the Sudan government.
Excluding a vast country endowed with huge natural resources from contemporary international affairs may not be the best strategy. As experience
has shown, isolating countries makes them conducive to violence, human
rights abuses and civil unrest.

China's huge presence in Sudan needs to be challenged on all fronts.
China must be made aware that its opportunistic involvement with dicta-
torship carries a price for trade and investment inside China. Support for
pro-democracy groups needs to be strengthened; investment that observes
acceptable international standards on the environment needs to be enhanced.
And above all, international justice mechanisms must be made more effective so that perpetrators know that eventually they will face justice.

*Ali Askouri is the director of the London based Piankhi Research Group working
in the field of development and human rights.*

Notes

1 Kuwait News Agency (Kuna) (2001) 7 April: 'During Ali Osman, Sudan Vice-president's visit, China had written off 63% of Sudan's 67.3 millions dollars debt, in addition to signing loan agreements to develop roads, scientific projects and electricity.'

2 Egypt and Ethiopia accused the government of Sudan and its Islamic group allies of carrying out the assassination attempt against the Egyptian president in Addis Ababa in June 1995, so the government of Sudan came under huge pressure to expel fundamentalist groups from their country. Much of these groups' investments were in agriculture and infrastructure (roads), both sectors which do not need particularly sophisticated technical know-how.

3 Sudan's voting rights in the International Monetary Fund (IMF were suspended in 1993. It was not until 2000, according to Agence France-Presse (AFP) (2000) 5 August, that the ' IMF lifted the seven-year suspension of Sudan's voting rights according to Dr. Mohamed Khair El Zubair, Sudanese minister of Finance. El Zubair said Sudan's foreign debts totalled US$20 billions, including $1.6 billion owed to the IMF. As a result the Minister expected that the international commercial, financial, and economic institutions would be willing to deal with Sudan.'

4 Human rights violations by the government of Sudan are well documented by human rights groups, such as Human Rights Watch and Amnesty International. Since 1994 the UN has had a special rapporteur to monitor human rights in Sudan.

5 Transparency International's corruption index for 2006, ranked the countries in which China is heavily involved as follows (the higher the number, the greater the level of corruption): out of 160 countries in the index, Ghana is ranked 73, Algeria 84, Ethiopia 134, Zimbabwe 137, Angola 142, Nigeria 146, Chad 157 and Sudan 159.

6 *Alray Al a'am Daily* (2006) 3 November. Sudanese unity, which China supports, was based on the hegemony of Muslims and Arabs groups in Sudan. The southern Sudanese have been fighting the central government for a secular state that accommodates all religions and races in the country, and to build a new Sudan based on equality. After about 50 years of civil war, the southern Sudanese will now have the right to self-determination, as stated in the Naivasha Agreement. If China continues its support for Sudanese unity, in disregard of the peace agreements, despite its rhetoric, it is supporting the resumption of war. However, despite the fact that China is taking sides in a very sensitive Sudanese internal matter, it still claims that it does not interfere in Sudan domestic affairs. The same is true of its position on UN peacekeeping forces in Darfur. In Sudan only the National Conference Party (the ruling party) is opposed to the UN peacekeeping forces. Again China claimed it was not interfering in domestic affairs!

7 In Sudan, the two main political parties, the Umma and the Democratic Unionist, are not part of the government. In addition, the National Popular Party, the Communist Party, the Ba'ath, and many other small parties are against the ruling National Conference Party.

8 See *Sudan Monthly Report* (1999) 15 October: ' the Deputy Head of the Sudanese diplomatic mission in Rome, Mr Altereife Kormino, said the truth is that there are only 6,000–7,000 Chinese protecting the pipeline. He refuted claims that the pipeline was under the surveillance of 20,000 specially trained Chinese militias.' See also Cleophas Lado (no date) 'The political economy of oil discovery and mining in Sudan: constraints and prospects on development' <http://www.dur.ac.uk/justin.willis/lado.htm>, who writes: 'Reports have surfaced that at least 2,000 of the Chinese labourers are prisoners who have been promised a reduction of their sentences in exchange for their labour. It has also been reported that 20,000 Chinese labourers, with probable military training, are planned to be used to protect China's investment in the oil project.'

9 Lado (no date).

10 Ibid.

11 Ibid.

12 Liquid Africa website, 16 July 2004.

13 The contract was signed in Khartoum in the Republican Palace in the presence of the president on 23 December 2003.

14 The name of the company could be Poli or Buli or Booli. Its form here is based on what appeared in the Arabic Sudanese newspaper *Al Sahafa Daily*, which did not provide the correct English name in the news item.

15 *Al Sahafa Daily* (2005) 25 April. *Al Sahafa* reported on 13 November 2006 that a contract for US$20 million was signed with a Chinese company to build the Al Diwaim bridge on the White Nile.

16 Ibid.

17 *Alray Al a'am Daily* (2006) 15 May.

18 Ibid.

19 *Alray Al a'm Daily* (2006) 4 October.

20 The website www.sudandevelopment.org (accessed 10 June 2006).

21 In July 2004 the United States Congress adopted a concurrent resolution condemning the atrocities in Darfur as 'genocide'.

22 Christian Aid (2001) *The Scorched Earth: Oil and War in Sudan*, <http://www.christian-aid. org.uk/indepth/0103suda/sudanoi2.htm#CHAP1>

23 Ibid. For more on oil and displacement see also John Ryle and Georgette Gagnoon (2001)

Report of Investigation into Oil Development, Conflict and Displacement in Western Upper Nile Sudan <http://www.vigilsd.org/Petrol/rep1001.html>. For the direct link between Chinese companies and oil displacement see also Human Rights Watch (2003) *Part II: Oil Fuels the War: Oil Development and Displacement in Block 5A, 1996 -98* <http://www.hrw.org/reports/2003/sudan1103/12.htm>.

24 The exact cost of the project is not known and the government is still looking for money to complete it. In a recent Arab Investments Forum held in Khartoum on 8–9 November 2006, the Merowe dam was presented by the government for finance along with other projects. According to *Alray Al a'm Daily* (27 October 2006), Finance State Minister Ahmed Al Magzoub told the Sudan News Agency that during the forum, major investment opportunities in hydropower generation would be presented and their respective feasibility studies would be made available. These opportunities would include, for instance, a set of dam projects: 'Sitait dam, Atabara River dam, Sheriak Dam, Kajabar dam, and Merowe dam project'.

25 <www.merowedam.com> accessed 17 November 2006.

26 See http://www.merowedam.com/en/structure.html. The contract was signed on 7 June 2003 in Khartoum by the chief executive of China Water Engineering (CWE), a member of the two Chinese companies making up the joint venture (*Alray Al a'm Daily*, 8 June 2003).

27 The contract was signed in the Republican Palace in the presence of the Sudanese president. The two Chinese companies were Harpin-Jilin and CCMD (Sudanese TV main newscast on 23 December 2003).

28 According to the dam authority, the project will displace three groups. These are the Hamdab group, representing 8 per cent of those displaced; the Amri group, 25 per cent; and the Manasir group, 67 per cent. For more see A. Askouri (2004) ' The Merowe Dam: controversy and displacment in Sudan', *Forced Migration Review*, 21 <http://fmo.qeh.ox.ac.uk/Repository/getPdf.asp?Path=FMR/1600/01/22&PageNo=1>.

29 http://www.sudaneseonline.com/cgibin/sdb/2bb.cgi?seq=msg&board=2&msg=1071347981&rn=1

30 P. Bosshard and N. Hildyard (2005) 'A Critical Juncture for Peace, Democracy and the Environment: Sudan and the Merowe Dam Project', a report from a visit to Sudan and a fact finding mission to the Merowe Dam Project, 22 February–1 March. A joint mission by Corner House (UK) and International River Network (USA) with Environmentalists Society (Sudan) <http://www.fmreview.org/FMRpdfs/FMR24/FMR2434.pdf>.

31 It was first called the Movement for Justice to the Forcibly Displaced Sudanese and for Building New Sudan (MJFDS), but later the name was changed to the Movement of the Displaced or MOD.

32 Movement of the Displaced (2004) 'Hamdab: The option for armed struggle', Press Release No. (1) 7 December, states ' Our land is our life, and when we set out to defend it, we are in fact defending our lives' <http://www.sudantribune.com/spip.php?article6881&var_recherche=Hamadab%20Dam>

33 Movement of the Displaced (2004) Press Statement No. (3), 10 December, issued as a response to the arrest of three members of the Manasir Executive Committee – Numeri Hasan Omar, Hassan Siddiq Atolabi and Al Nazir Omar Al Tahir – according to MOD. The MOD stated that the detainees were not members of the movement and that 'it has become clear that the security organ believes that, just being from the dam affected areas, warrants arrest'. The detainees remained in custody for about seven months and were released without charge on 30 June 2005, as reported by *Al Hayat* (a London based Arabic newspaper) on 1 July 2005.

34 The *Sudan Tribune* (2005) reported, 'Behind the current escalations is the Chinese contractors building the electrical network towers. The Chinese occupied water wells, preventing women and children from [collecting] water. The Chinese say they need the water for the concrete works and for their own domestic use in their camp', 29 November <http://www.sudantribune.com/spip.php?article12802&var_recherche=Hamadab%20Dam>.

35 *Sudan Tribune* (2005) 12 December.

36 See www.sudaneseonline.com/enews2006/apr23-75788.shtml. Those killed were: Atta Al Sayed Al Khidir Al Mahi (a farmer), Yassin Mohamed Al Khair (a farmer) and a third person whose details were not confirmed.

37 Sudan Human Rights, Cairo Organisation issued a strong statement of condemnation on 23 April 2006. The incident was also widely covered by many leading news agencies and satellites channels including Al Jazeera and Al Arabyia.

38 See Business and Human Rights Resource Centre (2006) 'Response of China International Water and Electic Corp. to concerns about shooting near Merowe Dam, Sudan' <http://www.business-humanrights.org/Search/SearchResults?SearchableText=Merowe+Dam>. Mr Ding States 'So far within our site no such event of what you mentioned in your e-mail occurred. Meanwhile we have not received any report from the project client, engineers and local government agencies on any of such events beyond the contractor's site.' This was on 12 May 2006, 20 days after the incident.

39 Ibid.

40 Lado (no date).

WIN-WIN ECONOMIC COOPERATION: CAN CHINA SAVE ZIMBABWE'S ECONOMY?

JOHN BLESSING KARUMBIDZA

The 'look east' policy of Zimbabwean president Robert Mugabe is well documented. But the deeper implications of Zimbabwe's relationship with China are less well understood. Whether the relationship turns out to be a win-win one will depend much on how effectively Zimbabwe can build institutional and bureaucratic capacity to harness Chinese funds and investment for the benefit of the country, writes John Blessing Karumbidza. He doubts whether this will be the case and raises questions as to whether Mugabe is simply replacing Western colonialism with Chinese imperialism.

We have turned east where the sun rises, and given our backs to the west, where the sun sets
Robert Mugabe on the occasion of the celebration of 25 years of Zimbabwean independence, May 2005

That China is a rising global economic player of note in Africa is well established. China's interest in Africa is part of a calculated plan and policy to 'go global'. Africa offers a strategic training ground and opportunity for Chinese capital. In an address to the Nigerian Senate in 2005, Chinese President described China-Africa relations as 'win-win economic cooperation'. This paper explores what will become of the renewed relationship between China and Zimbabwe, or more appropriately, the Zimbabwe African National Union, Patriotic Front (ZANU PF).

It is arguable that whether the relationship becomes what the Chinese president described as a 'win-win' relationship[1] is not entirely dependent on China, rather on whether Zimbabwe has the institutional and bureaucratic capacity to turn Chinese funds and investment to benefit the country. There are reasonable doubts about the possibility of widespread and long-term economic benefits to Zimbabwe. Temporary benefits so far include the political preservation of the Mugabe reign and personal aggrandisement through corruption and kickbacks by his ZANU PF cronies flowing from Chinese investment.

On the whole, it would not be fair to blame the Chinese for acting to further their interests. It is incumbent upon the government of Zimbabwe and its people (and any other African country for that matter) to put in place a programme and strategy for chanelling funds and direct investment in a way that contributes to the growth of its own economy.

Questions about Chinese financing and business involvement in African development programmes include: Are they based on an equal partnership? Are African governments able to negotiate terms of interaction without 'pawning' their countries and submitting their people to exploitation? It is the duty of the countries receiving foreign direct investment (FDI) and other forms of investments to attract appropriate labour intensive technology that helps create employment locally, and ensure that Chinese labour practices in Africa conform to local labour laws.

There is growing concern that China disregards human rights and democracy. It has a reputation for the abuse of workers' rights, intolerance of political opposition and dislikes a free press. In the name of non-interference, China justifies doing business with pariah states and dictators – which also means that civil society and the citizenry cannot hold them accountable for flaunting environmental and labour laws. Lindsey Hilsum cited the Sierra Leonean ambassador to Beijing, who explained why China has been able to dominate the African business space:

> The Chinese are doing more than the G8 in making poverty history. If a G8 country had wanted to rebuild the stadium, we'd still be holding meetings. The Chinese just come and do it. They don't hold meetings about environmental impact assessment, human rights, bad governance and good governance. I'm not saying it's right, just that Chinese investment is succeeding because they don't set high benchmarks. [2]

It is important to note, however, that this Chinese 'non-interference' policy cannot be permanent. The Chinese are well aware of this themselves.

Where deals are signed with unpopular dictatorial regimes that could later be revised by a new government, it becomes necessary for the Chinese to protect such regimes. This explains their arming of the ZANU PF government in Zimbabwe. For example, China funded Zimbabwe's acquisition of military-strength radio jamming equipment to block opposition broadcasts ahead of the 2005 elections.[3]

According to Juan Jose Daboub, the World Bank's managing director, 'Chinese handouts without reforms will not help receiving countries'. He argues for the Bank's approach of working 'next to the country, shar[ing] experiences, show[ing] by virtue of example of other countries that certain things work'.[4] It is the case, however, that this same bank and Western approach over the past half century has failed to deliver development, and left Africa in more debt that when they began.

Liberation ties paying off for China

In seeking to gain a hold on African resources and opportunities for the sale of Chinese goods, China should be wary of losing the political capital and 'credibility' it acquired from supporting African liberation struggles through conniving with dictatorial regimes. Prior to the present day questionable expansion, China had no burden of historical guilt in Africa, unlike the global North. China therefore gives credence to the likes of Mugabe when it claims to be protecting African sovereignty. Whereas European colonial rule left tribal strife leading to wars that destroyed infrastructure, the Chinese have rebuilt infrastructure.[5] Whereas British Prime Minister Tony Blair and Bono see Africa as a 'scar on everyone's conscience', still troubled by their historical guilt of the slave and colonial era, the Chinese see Africa as a business opportunity. This is confirmed by evidence everywhere: Chinese lumberjacks in the Central African Republic, Chinese textiles in Lesotho, Chinese tourists in Zimbabwe, Chinese newspapers in South Africa, Chinese geologists in Sudan, Chinese channels on African satellite television.[6]

> Almost every African country today bears examples of China's emerging presence: from oil fields in the east, to farms in the south, and mines in the centre of the continent.[7]

According to a recent Reuters report, Chinese-run farms in Zambia supply the vegetables sold in Lusaka's street markets, and Chinese companies – in addition to launching Nigerian satellites – have a virtual monopoly on the construction business in Botswana.[8]

Addressing the Nigerian House of Assembly in April 2006, the Chinese president sounded like a World Bank official praising globalisation's 'profound and complex changes' in the world and claiming that:

> Peace, development and cooperation are the calling of the times. Thanks to accelerated economic globalization, countries are becoming increasingly interdependent and their interests more closely interconnected. Working together to share opportunities, meet challenges and achieve common development is the desire of all peoples.[9]

In the same address, the Chinese president proudly narrated how 'great progress in China-Africa relations over the past 50 years will remain fresh in our minds' and reminded listeners that 'as far back as the Bandung Conference in 1955, a New China and African leaders … met and shook hands'. China helped Africa to train freedom fighters for national liberation. And African countries supported the restoration of the lawful seat of the People's Republic of China in the UN. Braving hardship in the tropical jungles, Chinese and African workers built the great Tanzam railway. The railway line helped to link Tanzania and Zambia, creating a communication escape from the Western economy and its local agent, South Africa. Fifty years later, China has recommitted itself to building a new type of Asian-African strategic partnership, and the recent inauguration of China–Africa cooperation paves the way for a stronger 'partnership'.

The earlier 'ideological' phase of Chinese-African relations was part of a global strategy which by the mid 1970s saw some 15,000 doctors and over 10,000 agricultural engineers from China serving all over the Third World. It is common knowledge that many African countries exploited the cold war and the bi-polar world system by claiming to be socialist to gain assistance during liberation and after independence, going first to the West, then the East for development aid.

Soon after his election, Namibian President Hifikepunye Pohamba acknowledged the historical and long-standing tradition of friendship between his country and China, praising the Chinese government and people as having 'given firm and sincere support to the Namibian people during their struggle for independence and in their cause of national construction thereafter'. More than 25,000 Chinese families now live in Namibia, allegedly part of the economic and cultural exchange deal, although the Namibian government refutes the assertion.

By 1977 Chinese trade with Africa reached a record US$817 million. The new orientation found institutional expression in the first China-Africa Co-operation Forum held in Beijing in 2000 – a mechanism to promote diplomatic relations, trade and investment between China and African countries. In the same year, China-Africa trade passed US$10bn for first time. By 2003 it reached US$18.5 billion. By 2004, nearly 700 Chinese companies were operating in 49 African countries. According to some estimates US$30 billion will change between Chinese and African hands this year. More recent Chinese estimates claim that it is already approaching US$40 billion.

Africa has rich resources and market potential, whereas China brings effective practices and know-how it has gained in the course of modernisation. China has the capacity to develop knowledge-based cooperation such as capacity building, human resources training and science and technology exchanges; to promote value-added processing of primary products; to upgrade traditional industries; and to enhance social development for local communities.

China is using the UN's five-point proposal to 'assist' developing countries accelerate development, including: 'Granting zero-tariff treatment for some exports from the least developed countries, increasing aid to the heavily-indebted poor countries and least developed countries and cancelling debts contracted by them, providing concessional loans and effective medicine for treating malaria, and training professionals.'

These steps will increase China's access to the raw materials, energy and food resources it requires to sustain growth as well as feed its population. Observers have pointed to the fact that 'more recently China's policy has shifted from cold war ideology to a more classical pursuit of economic self-interest in the form of access to raw materials, markets and spheres of influence through investment, trade and military assistance – to the point where China can be suspected of pursuing the goals of any classical imperialist'.[10] Moreover, the heavy militarisation of the Zimbabwean government through Chinese loans and technology raises suspicions of China's global ambitions to develop strategic military bases in Africa.

The nature and character of Chinese investment

For Mugabe, who sees democracy and development as mutually exclusive, the fact that China has been able to raise 400 million of its people out of poverty over two decades, without being subjected to democratic elections and a free press serves as a useful example. Mugabe cites the present world order as a source of conflict and war, and calls for a more positive alternative order. He sees 'China as an alternative global power point', which could form 'the foundation of a new global paradigm'. Despite the fact the majority of Chinese nationals are excluded from this growth, and many rebellions are recorded regularly, he has committed Zimbabwe to working for this new paradigm, founded on principles of 'sovereignty and independence'.[11]

China was ZANU PF's main supporter in the 1970s in the war against colonial rule. After independence, Zimbabwe declared itself Marxist-Leninist and announced the intention to reorganise society along socialist lines while courting Western aid and the IMF.[12,13]

Since 1980, Zimbabwe has revoked its liberation era ties with China to maintain low profile diplomatic connections, which are now upgraded to a development partnership. As a result of the lack of conditionalities on Chinese loans and funding, Chinese loans in the 1980s went into white elephant projects, such as the construction of the National Stadium.

By the end of 2004, Chinese investments in Zimbabwe were estimated at US$600 million. To service the increasing Chinese investment and the 9,000 Chinese believed to be living and working in Zimbabwe a bi-weekly flight between Harare and Beijing was launched.[14] Another US$600 million was pledged at the June 2005 Asia summit, and separate deals between Chinese state and private firms were signed with various Zimbabwean corporations (see Table 1). Renewed and closer China–Zimbabwe relations brought about

familiar circumstances: a Zimbabwean state now considere
North as a pariah state; an unprecedented economic slump;
above 75 per cent, inflation heading towards 2,000 per cent; and shortages
of consumer goods, most importantly fuel.

Table 1 Chinese involvement in non-agricultural sectors of the Zimbabwean economy

Sector	Projects	Deal status	Source
Mining in copper, platinum, gold and diamonds	Mhangura Copper Mine (closed in 2000 because of poor copper prices) Hwange Colliery Company (HCC) (construction of 3 thermal power stations) Chrome mining	Signed Chinese Aero-technology Import and Export Company (CATIC) and Zimbabwe Mining Development Corporation (ZMDC) worth US$400m, June 2006. China North Industries Corporation (NORINCO) takes over to defer for 2 years a US$6.3m owed by HCC. Worth US$70m The Guardian placed mining and energy deals at £700m China's Star Communications funded by China Development Bank Asian Summit June 2006 committed £700m	BBC, 12 June 2006 Zimbabwe Independent, 4 November 2006 Zimbabwe Standard, 5 November 2006 The Guardian, 16 June 2006

| Electricity Utility, ZESA | Hwange Power Station refurbishment (requires US$37m)

Kariba South Extension (requires US$200m) | Expected to kick off once Zimbabwe Electricity Regulatory Commission (ZERC) and the government have decided between CATIC, Iranian Electrical and Construction Company (FARAB) and Global Steel, which have been short-listed for different parts of the projects | The Herald, 28 September 2006 The Zimbabwean, The Independent, The Guardian |
|---|---|---|---|
| National railways | | Supply and servicing of passenger trains | Herald, 15 June 2006 |
| Broadcasting | Equipment | Zimbabwe Broadcasting Cooperation | Herald, 15 June 2006 |
| Telephone & communication | Tel-One

Telecoms equipment

Communications monitoring & transmission blocking equipment | Huawei (a technology firm) has a US$440m contract to supply telecom equipment | BBC News, 22 Nov 2004 Zim-Online, 6 Nov 2006, The UK Herald, 31 March 2005 |
Construction	Border posts, airports, bridges		Herald, 15 June 2006
IT, industrial & military hardware	Scanners & aviation	Passenger planes, fighter jets and weapons	The Guardian, 16 June 2006
Steel industry	Zimbabwe Iron and Steel Corporation (ZISCO)	Renewal of and construction of new furnaces	Herald, 15 June 2006
Bilateral trade		Hit US$100m by June 2006	Herald, 15 June 2006

Note: This table was compiled from a randomly selected variety of sources as indicated in column 4.

European and American travel sanctions, the lack of any IMF rating, coupled with the South African ANC's conditions of political and economic 'normalisation' have taken their toll. In August 2005 therefore, snubbing the efforts of Thabo Mbeki, Mugabe turned to China for funding to 'revive the economy through increased agricultural production'. This led to Chinese promises for increased economic cooperation in many areas of the economy and an immediate US$2 million to finance agricultural production and three MA-60 passenger planes. Industry and International Trade Minister Obert Mpofu described the deal as being an:

> 'All-weather relations' with China, both at the economic and political level, but it has become more imperative now for us to grow our economic ties for mutual benefit. This is particularly so given that we are reforming our economy, and China is doing the same' adding that 'we have increased our economic cooperation, we are going in the future on the basis of agreements like [those which] have been signed with the Chinese Eximbank to finance inputs such as fertiliser. China is keen to secure strategic natural resources to help sustain its mouth-watering economic growth of more than 10 percent, is investing heavily in agriculture and mining in Zimbabwe where Chinese investment is now estimated to be billions of dollars.[15]

For Mugabe, such investment was welcomed as reducing Zimbabwe's vulnerability to the pressure and political manipulation of the West.

Mugabe fought the 2005 elections on the argument that Zimbabwe must not become a colony again. But it is questionable whether he has not in fact simply replaced Western colonialism with Chinese imperialism. The ceding of control of strategic state firms and massive Chinese takeovers, including of railways, the electricity supply, Air Zimbabwe and Zimbabwe Broadcasting Corporation make 'win-win' economic cooperation between China and Zimbabwe appear doubtful.[16]. Given that Zimbabwe has no comparative advantage over China in any sector, this opening up of the economy is most likely to benefit the Chinese perhaps even at the expense of Zimbabweans.[17]

Zimbabwe lacks the institutional and strategic infrastructure to effect requisite economic transformation and will have difficulty putting Chinese development loans to good use. The failure to revive the agriculture sector since the 2000 land seizures is a major concern. This failure has a precedent. Following independence in 1980, Zimbabwe failed to transform the African agricultural sector from subsistence production, short term increases in maize and cotton output not withstanding. Rather, the new regime retained the notion that large-scale white farmers were more productive than Africans. This was in spite of the international donor support and an ena-bling global environment.

It is not surprising therefore that the Chinese signed a contract to farm 386 square miles of land when millions of Zimbabweans are still landless.[18] Recent land seizures saw most of the productive land fall into the hands

---

British Prime Minister Tony Blair and Bono see Africa as a 'scar on everyone's conscience', while the Chinese see Africa as a business opportunity.

---

of the elite, while the rural poor remain mostly landless. The Reserve Bank governor's monetary policy statement emphasised the need for the agri-culture sector to pull its weight in the economic turnaround of the country, encouraging the new landowners (mostly urban 'telephone farmers') that 'the battle cry is for all those who hold land to view it as an effective means of economic emancipation rather than a status symbol'.

Addressing the Zimbabwe Fertilizer Company (ZFU) in Chinhoyi recently, Vice-President Joyce Mujuru berated the new 'farmers' calling them the enemies of progress for failing to 'feed themselves and let alone the country'. She also reported the launch of Operation Maguta, a programme where 'the army has taken over huge swathes of former white-owned land in a desperate attempt to produce strategic crops such as maize and wheat' in response to food shortages.[19] Thus governor Gono's assertion that 'land reform is a closed chapter' in the face of this farming failure, food shortages and land hunger is an act of political delusion.

Table 2 Chinese involvement in Zimbabwean agricultural revival

Agriculture	Project status	Source
Fertilisers	200,000 to 400,000 tonnes of fertiliser	People's Daily, 14 Nov 2006
	Already 22,000 delivered by 1 November 2006	Herald, 8 November 2006
	Deal singed between the ZFC but Grain Marketing Board (GMB) laboratory tests have led to the condemnation of 160 tonnes as unsustainable	
Equipment	Transfer of tractors, trucks and other machinery needed for farming	
Direct farming	A contract deal through which Chinese farmers have been allocated 386 square miles of land	Taipei Times, 28 July 2005
Trade	Zimbabwe is expected to export beef to China	People's Daily, 21 Sep 2006

Beyond the rhetoric of 'the land being the economy and the economy the land' there is no apparent strategy for the necessary transformation required for agriculture to release it potential for the economic turnaround needed in Zimbabwe. Zimbabwe cannot even benefit from the Chinese Maoist blueprint for rural economic transformation.[20] The joint Chinese ventures in Zimbabwean agriculture amount to nothing more than land renting and typical agri-business relations that turn the land holders and their workers into labour tenants and subject them to exploitation.

James Jowa, a Harare-based economist, observed: 'it is understandable that with frosty relations with the West, Zimbabwe seeks alternative economic partners, but the big question is what have we benefited or what will we benefit from them?'[21] One of the major factors in answering this question is whether Zimbabwe has the capacity to execute the deals from paper to reality.

The duplication of deals between China and Russia on related projects point to either the reckless desperation for any loan available or the failure of the Zimbabwean bureaucracy to manage such huge joint ventures. The reports of corruption involving the awarding of tenders and signing of deals, for instance the Steel Firm scandal involving Zimbabwe Iron and Steel Corporation (ZISCO) and Global Steel (an Indian-based company), and the lavishness with which this 'easy-come-no-strings' Chinese money is being spent are major concerns.[22]

Mugabe is known to have bought the senior policy and army officers another fleet of luxury cars, in quick succession after those bought in 2004, which they have been allowed to retain.[23] Instead of loans, Zimbabwe's hope probably lies in attracting FDI as loans in an economy that is not functional,

---

the Chinese president sounded like a World Bank official praising globalisation's 'profound and complex changes'

---

lacking hard currency, riddled with fuel and food shortages, has a high rate of skills turnover and runaway inflation will increase the indebtedness of the country and arrest the potential even for economic revival. There is no clear indication how the loans will be repaid and this could be because the Chinese bank on what they will get out of the mineral deposits.

However, whatever happens, many generations to come are going to be paying back these Chinese, Russian and Indian loans. According to *Xinhua*[24] China intends to double its assistance to Africa by 2009, providing US$3 billion dollars of preferential loans and US$2 billion of preferential buyer's credits, establishing a special fund of US$5 billion to encourage Chinese investment in Africa and cancelling debts owed by certain heavily-indebted or least developed African countries that have diplomatic ties in Africa. Maybe this way, the Zimbabwean debts will be 'forgiven' provided there are still mineral resources to be mined. Gavin Du Venage of *The Australian*[25] reported the souring of relations between Zimbabwe and China as a series of bills remained unpaid for aircraft, engineering work and construction projects leading to a number of Chinese firms suspending work. These projects resumed after Zimbabwe negotiated another loan in June 2006, demonstrating an attitude of repaying debts by incurring more debt.

There is additional fear that the takeover of strategic national firms by the

Chinese companies is a security threat and can be seen as loss of national sovereignty. Most sinister of all is that the Chinese authorities must know that Zimbabwe is more than likely to default on payment of bills, and wishes precisely this, in order to obtain a tighter grip on Zimbabwean assets.

It would be naïve to think that China is motivated by the need to salvage the Zimbabwean economy from its economic abyss; indeed even the government does not itself believe this. It is simply a venture to save political face. For the Chinese, the investment in Zimbabwe is nothing different from Chinese ventures elsewhere on the continent. The current arrangements simply allow Mugabe to keep the illusion of victory over the West and enable his cronies in the army, police, government and business to partner with the Chinese in further exploitation of the masses. As in the 1980s, the poor people will be told to tie their stomachs and pull up their socks, and that a revolution is not for 'cry babies'. For as long as Mugabe reigns over the abyss, the rhetoric of imperialist demons fighting against Zimbabwe will continue to suffice.

In the context of a politicised security system, silenced media and partial judiciary, the Chinese will drain the Zimbabwean economy and future generations will pay for it.

However, this does not mean that there is no voice against the obvious takeover of the economy by the Chinese. Abusive phrases used by many, such as 'fong kong' in South Africa and 'zhing zhong' in Zimbabwe can be considered expressions of general displeasure about the poor quality and flooding of Chinese products.

Attitudes towards the Chinese

South Africa has been fighting a losing battle against crime in general but the Chinese took exception to the fact that more than 40 armed robbery cases, leading to eight fatalities, were recorded with Chinese victims in 2002 and 'three Chinese business people were killed by armed robbers within 36 hours'. The Chinese investors called for China and South Africa to take more effective measures to guarantee their personal and property safety. The general manager of a Chinese import and export company with an annual trade volume of more than US$10 million told *Xinhua*:

If our personal safety cannot be guaranteed, how can we continue to carry out business there? We are very concerned about the recent attacks, and we fear that the poor security situation in South Africa will have a negative impact on our business there. We are still willing to expand our scope of business in South Africa, and I hope the South African government will also take effective measures to ensure that the life and property security of the Chinese business people is guaranteed.[26]

The official response by Vusi B. Koloane, minister plenipotentiary of the South African embassy in China, that the South African government was increasing safety budgets, police forces and international cooperation to make South Africa a 'zero-crime' country. Not wanting to be outdone by the South African minster of security, who invited the 'whingers' to leave the country, Koloane suggested that 'South Africa does not have as bad a crime record as some media have reported' adding that 'it is one of the leading countries in the world in terms of safety, which does not discriminate on the basis of colour, gender or age'.[27]

When confronted with reports of crime against Chinese nationals (numbering not more than 10,000), Zimbabwe established a Chinese desk at the central police station in Harare. Mugabe has also appointed a minister for Chinese affairs.

Already, the police officers, the University of Zimbabwe and schools have been asked to offer classes in Mandarin (soon after losing their love of French). Reacting to the new requirement to learn Mandarin, Washington Katema, ZINASU president, snubbed the move as a case of the 'madness of the Mugabe regime scaling new heights' and as a political gimmick to lure the Chinese into the country to bankroll the bankrupt regime.[28] These excesses by Mugabe's regime are likely to fuel xenophobia against the Chinese. Many reports of crime and abuse of women and children, rape and violent crimes against Zimbabwean nationals are yet to receive such a high profile response.

The economic background to the anti-Chinese sentiments is that Zimbabweans are horrified at the prospect of a permanent take-over of strategic state companies in what is generally considered a desperate move to perpetuate the tenure of ZANU PF. Trade unionists are worried that companies are being forced to close, having lost their market to cheaper goods imported directly from China, and about the abuse of workers.[29] The Chinese managers are alleged to have a negative attitude towards local people and massive dislike for trade unionists. At will they are known to 'forget' to understand English as a means to avoid dialogue with anyone critical of their actions. The Zimbabwe Congress of Trade Unions (ZCTU) was quoted as saying that a Chinese steel company operating in Willowvale in Harare has unacceptable pollution levels but the government treats them with kid gloves.[30]

In part, Zimbabweans' attitudes towards the Chinese are because they find it difficult to identify the specific benefits of Chinese economic partnership. Mugabe's palace is roofed with donated Chinese tiles and his wife has a new destination for shopping. For the Chinese, Mugabe is candidate for an honorary professorship in international relations, conferred by the Chinese

---

more recently China's policy has shifted from cold war ideology to a more classical pursuit of economic self-interest

---

Foreign Affairs University in honour of the 'remarkable contribution in the work of diplomacy and international relations by his Excellency'.[31] The job of checking the quality of Chinese goods is in the hands of the Standards Association of Zimbabwe (SAZ), but as with any parastatals, the officials dare not reject cheap Chinese goods against the will of Mugabe, who is known to rage against any official who challenges him. However, there is some evidence that the Zimbabwean people realise that 'Chinese goods are not good for their economy.'[32]

Free-for-all or ground for global capital novices?

Chinese firms are needing to rethink their attitudes and business ethics in Zimbabwe as they now face the challenge of Russia, India and Iran, who have also rushed to the party to pick some crumbs from Zimbabwe's free-

---

Mugabe's looking 'east where the sun rises',
expecting Chinese loans to develop the beleaguered
economy remains a fantasy as long as his
politics and economics are wrong.

---

falling economy. Recently, Russia has begun to restore its African presence – a move demonstrated by President Vladimir Putin's visit to Africa and the southern sub-region. Russia's RusAviaTrade, an investment company, has placed bids worth US$400 million in various sectors including mining, tourism, electricity and construction projects. This follows a recent visit by a 48-member Russian delegation, including 17 journalists, to Zimbabwe and duplicates areas of Chinese interest, thus confusing the Zimbabwean government which obviously lacks the complexity to deal with situations like this. A floodgate of corruption, backhand dealings and kickbacks resulted, which lead to the freezing of many of the deals already signed.[33]

The Indians are not to be outdone. As their economy grows, the prospect of increasing raw material and market share has also encouraged ventures in Africa, particularly in Zimbabwe. India's Global Steel increased its bid for the Zimbabwe Iron and Steel Corporation (ZISCO) from US$171 million to US$400 million to outdo the Chinese, and then replaced a local manager with an Indian executive. However, the deal is still frozen, as it has become a huge corruption scandal – dubbed Steelgate, which is at the centre of the succession battle within ZANU PF.[34]

Conclusion

In the next half century if all African countries abandoned the colonial languages which create a barrier to cultural unity, China could replace them with one language spoken across the continent. Maybe then, a 'United States of Africa' – under Chinese 'prefectship' – would become possible. After all, China would gain more from a united Africa than from a balkanised continent. China is in Africa to pursue expansion, consistent with its search for global dominance, and to avoid being out-competed by the US. It therefore requires resources, raw materials, and markets, and space for its surplus population.

As far as Africa is concerned, however, as long as poverty remains at the centre of the conflicts and crises in Africa, and there is no African reconstruction and development strategy, conceived and funded from local resources, the giant panda will carry on from where the colonialists and imperialists left.

Mugabe's looking 'east where the sun rises', expecting Chinese loans to develop the beleaguered economy, remains a fantasy as long as his politics and economics are wrong. Meanwhile, with Mugabe fixated on Chinese promises, the people of Zimbabwe, especially the middle class that decide to abandon the country to the whims of Mugabe, and the Chinese take over while they pursue temporary respite in the diaspora, only have themselves to blame.

John (Blessing) Karumbidza is an economic historian and researcher in rural sociology based at the University of KwaZulu-Natal in South Africa. He is a public intellectual who is seeking to promote the position that 'another Afrika is possible'.

Notes

1 Hu Jintao (President of the People's Republic of China) (2006) 'Work Together to Forge a New Type of China-Africa Strategic Partnership', address to the National Assembly of Nigeria. 27 April <http://jm.chineseembassy.org/eng/xw/t259668.htm>.

2 L. Hilsum (2005) 'The Chinese are Coming'. *New Statesman* 4 July <http://www.newstatesman.com/200507040007>.

3 I. Bruce (2005) 'China Aids Mugabe's Move to Silence Rivals', *The Herald* [Scotland, UK] 31 March <www.theherald.co.uk/36371.shtml>.

4 G. Bell (2006) China '"Handouts" No Route to Success – World Bank', *Reuters*, 7 November <http://www.alertnet.org/thenews/newsdesk/L07318580.htm>.

5 L. Beck (2006) 'China in Africa: Boon or Burden?' *Reuters*, 5 November <http://www.alertnet.org/thenews/newsdesk/PEK279942.htm>.

6 *Mail & Guardian* (2006) April 7.

7 P. Mooney (2005) 'China's African Safari', *Yale Global*, 3 January

<http://yaleglobal.yale.edu/article.print?id=5106>.

8 G. Bell (2006).

9 Hu Jintao (2006).

10 S Marks (2006) 'China in Africa: The New Imperialism?' <http://www.pambazuka.org/en/category/features/32432>.

11 P. Goodenough (2003) 'Mugabe Envisages Alternative World Order Headed by China', *CNSNews.com*, 3 December.

12 P. Bond (1988) *Uneven Zimbabwe: A Study of Finance, Development and Underdevelopment.* Trenton: Africa World Press.

13 M. Manyana and P. Bond (2202) *Zimbabwe's Plunge: Exhausted Nationalism, Neoliberalism and the Search for Social Justice.* Trenton: University of KwaZulu-Natal Press, Merlin Press, Weaver Press and Africa World Press.

14 *BBC News* (2006) 22 November.

15 *Xinhua* (2006) 'China Concerned About Crimes Against Nationals', 9 February <http://news.xinhuanet.com/english/2006-02/09/content_4159791.htm>.

16 C. Shoko (2006) 'It's Official – Zimbabwe is Sold to China', 24 October <http://www.changezimbabwe.com>.

17 *Xinhua* (2006) 'China Concerned About Crimes Against Nationals', 9 February.

18 *Taipei Times* (2005) 'China Greets Mugabe With Open Arms', 28 July <www.taipeitimes.com/News/world/archives/2005/07/28/2003265364>.

19 *Zim-Online* (2006) 'Vice-President Rebukes Black Farmers', 4 November <http://www.zimonline.co.za/Article.aspx?ArticleId=413>.

20 *Zimbabwe Independent* (2006) 10 November.

21 *Mail and Guardian Online* (2006) 10 November.

22 B. Zulu (2006) *Voice of America*, 8 November.

23 *The Zimbabwean* (2006) 9 November.

24 *Xinhua* (2006) 14 November.

25 G. Du Venage (2006) 'China Yet to See Mugabe's Cash', *The Australian* 23 May < www.theaustralian.news.com.au/>.

26 *Xinhua* (2006) 'China Concerned About Crimes Against Nationals', 9 February.

27 *Xinhua* (2006) 4 October.

28 B. Peta (2006) 'Zim Students Not Keen to Saying "Howzit, China"'. *The Star*, 26 January.

29 C. Shoko (2006).

30 'SW Radio Africa' (2006) *Zimbabwe News*, 14 November.

31 *Taipei Times* (2005).

32 M. Mugabe (2006) 'Who Wants the Chinese?' 14 November <http://74.52.38.210/
~makusha1/index.php?option=com_content&task=view&id=196&Itemid=2>.

33 *Zimbabwe Independent* (2006) 20 October.

34 ZANU PF (2006) *Zimbabwe Standard*, 7 November.

CHINA'S GRAND RE-ENTRANCE INTO AFRICA – MIRAGE OR OASIS?

MOREBLESSINGS CHIDAUSHE

Moreblessings Chidaushe tackles the issue of development aid to Africa, comparing the approach of the West and the new player, China. What is significantly different, she states, is that instead of the top-down language used by the West, China has instead used language that speaks of partnership and friendship. The West should not see China as a threat to its hold over Africa. Africa should be left to decide who it wants to engage with, she concludes.

Introduction

In recent years China, has gone out of its way to make intensive, deliberate efforts to rekindle its relationship with Africa – making a grand re-entrance into the continent after keeping a low profile through the 1980s. To date China has established firm relations with 48 of the 53 African countries. Our 'newest' eastern friends are fast establishing themselves in all the strategic economic sectors of the continent – from cheap quality low priced corner shops to gigantic mining, oil, and other infrastructural projects from Cape to Cairo.

This 'grand re-entrance' is stirring mixed reactions, covering the whole range from excitement to panic, disappointment and uncertainty; and not just from Africans but from the whole international community.

The African leadership sees this rekindled relationship as a golden opportunity to escape Western domination and make the West less relevant to Africa. But Africa's people have yet to see if they or just the leadership will benefit from this relationship.

The West complains that China is not genuinely concerned for Africa, so much as for its raw materials. The international financial institutions (IFIs), to whom Africa is heavily indebted, complain that China's involvement in Africa undermines good governance and will only lead to a deepened debt and governance crisis.

China has avoided the intrusive political governance conditionalities associated with Western aid and boasted of its non-interference policy, claiming a horizontal rather than a top-bottom approach. This approach has led countries such as Angola, Sudan and Zimbabwe to shun the IFIs and the rest of the donor world. When their relations sour, other African countries may follow. But only time will tell whether China is indeed a better partner than the West and if Western concerns are justified.

This article interrogates China's new approach to Africa in the specific context of development aid (grants, loans, technical experts). It seeks to compare the Chinese approach to that of Western donors and analyse the extent to which it benefits Africa.

Is China actually offering Africa a better development aid option than the West? Will Chinese aid move Africa towards achieving the Millennium Development Goals (MDGs)? Is China a new friend or a new imperialist? What will be the West's role in this new paradigm? And most importantly is this engagement just a case of whose turn it is to colonise the continent?

Background

Chinese–African relations date back to 1956, when China first established diplomatic relations with Egypt. To date, it has established relations with 48 African countries. But the present phase of Chinese involvement can be dated to around 2000 with the hosting in Beijing of the first ministerial conference of the Forum on China-Africa Cooperation, which received massive participation from the African partners.

The forum principle was based on 'carrying out consultation on an equal footing, enhancing understanding, increasing consensus, promoting friendship and furthering cooperation'. China's apparently gentle and appealing attitude coupled with growing concerns and restlessness about a largely unproductive engagement with the West served to strengthen the relationship. But China's growing superpower ambitions have also led to more assertive efforts to strengthen this relationship especially around Africa's strategic resource endowments. These efforts culminated in the policy announced in January 2006.

China's policy on Africa

In January 2006, China unveiled its new policy on Africa, an all-round, coherent roadmap articulating China's objectives and strategies in areas ranging from high-level exchange visits and consultation mechanisms to trade and investment, finance and agriculture, resources, tourism coopera-tion, infrastructure, debt relief and cooperation in human resources devel-opment, science and technology, cultural exchanges and much more. The policy is a well thought out articulation of China's strategic interests on the continent and the mechanisms to achieve them.

One of its most striking features is its friendly language and 'soft power' approach. It repeatedly emphasises such themes as mutually beneficial cooperation, friendly relations, fresh opportunities, sincerity, equality, mutual support, common prosperity. It projects a gentle, friendly, caring attitude, which appears to many Africans as a welcome contrast with the exploitation and heavy handed top-down relationship which has typified the West's approach. The presence of nearly all African leaderships at the recent Beijing summit is one sign of this.

However, while China has a clear policy to engage with Africa as a whole, Africa's approach to China still remains largely ad hoc. Although several countries have adopted a 'Look East' policy, these are still at individual

---

It projects a gentle, friendly, caring attitude, which appears to many Africans as a welcome contrast with the exploitation and heavy handed, top-down relationship which has typified the West's approach.

---

national levels with each country pursuing maximum benefit for its own best interests and specific needs.

But without a comprehensive and structured policy, will African countries be equipped to deal with this increasingly powerful friend without being short-changed? The relationship is supposedly an 'equal' partnership. But logic and experience suggest that it is impossible to engage on an equal footing as long as the parties are not on the same level. China is coming in as a donor and Africa as a recipient, much as it has been with the West.

The scales are thus already tipped in China's favour making it difficult for Africa to bargain a genuine partnership. While this might be slightly different to the traditional Western domination, it is still a form of domination.

It is sobering to point out that the benefit from Chinese aid is minimal. For example the proposed 100 schools will only translate to two schools per country in a continent whose member countries need more than 100 schools each.

Africa is undoubtedly desperate both for resources and to break free from the West and collaborate with the Chinese. Without strategic engagement, this desperation may expose Africa to manipulation by China.

China's stance on Africa is likely to harden in the long term, with more manipulation and exploitation and less benefit for the continent. The soft stance remains as long as China is settling in. One way out would be the development of a comprehensive African policy on China. This would result in more structured, secure and beneficial engagement and indeed potentially create the platform for a true 'win-win situation'.

An African policy on China would have to be developed through a continental body such as the African Union with multi-stakeholder collaboration at all levels, beginning at grassroots and feeding into regional blocks like SADC (Southern Africa), EAC (East Africa), ECOWAS (West Africa).

Such a policy would increase African countries' security and make it easier for them to deal with the superpower wannabe rather than making individual approaches that are easily susceptible to manipulation. Others might argue that different national interests would call for different policies and engagement mechanisms with China. Under such circumstances, individual countries could well be encouraged to develop their national policies on China within the framework of a complementary continental policy.

It is sobering to point out that benefit from the Chinese aid is minimal. For example the proposed 100 schools will only translate to two schools per country in a continent whose member countries need more than 100 schools each. The same applies for the proposed 100 agricultural experts to be sent to Africa and the 50 clinics. It is therefore still crucial for Africa to maintain good relations with other partners. A huge concern is that currently China and Western relations with Africa are being approached from a competitive point of view. A way should be sought to combine these efforts to maximise the benefit for Africa.

Development aid in Africa

A look at the UN (the world's largest development agency) will show the remarkable successes aid has achieved since the organisation's inception in a range of areas including child survival, environmental protection, complex emergencies and disaster situations, human rights, education, agricultural development and peace. In itself, aid is a good and desirable thing and can assist in minimising the suffering of those in difficult circumstances and in having a positive impact on the lives of those in need. The problem arises when objectives are distorted by other strategic political and economic motivations as is currently the case.

The crisis of Western aid has been that the more the industry has grown, the more distorted it has become and the more detached from reality. Strategic dynamics have grown to undermine the fundamentals of aid. Several decades and billions of dollars down the line, frustration and criticism around the effectiveness of Western aid have grown especially amongst the intended beneficiaries. The concern is that there is a rather weak link between the aid intentions, amounts poured into development and the worsening situation on the ground.

It is no wonder projects like the Reality of Aid (ROA) question why despite billions of dollars poured into Africa, more than half of the continent still lives below the poverty line. In fact more people are poor today because of development aid than they were 25 years ago. It is also no wonder that when a new player like China comes in with what seems to be an olive branch, Africa is more than ready to embrace it as long as it so much as promises to offer something better.

China and development aid

Critics and even development practitioners themselves have long recommended that Africa needs more grants than loans, less technical aid, cheap loans and aid without conditionalities and they have also called for more trade rather than aid. This section examines the extent to which Chinese aid is actually meeting these recommendations.

China is itself a developing country – in fact the largest developing country in the world. It shares with Africa a similar history of exploitation and domination by the West. But it got freedom earlier and adopted an aggressive approach to its development. Because it has not depended on aid to the same extent as Africa, it has achieved impressive development in the past 50 years.

It is no wonder Africa is ready to embrace engagement with China as it considers the country to have crucial experience from which Africa can learn. China chooses to concentrate on the huge infrastructural investments, production and trade, and investments – and less on charity and the social sectors – and the turnover from these have proved more beneficial than development aid. Having called for more trade than aid, Africa is therefore more likely to benefit from China's approach, which differs significantly from the West's.

But it is critical for Africa to be cautious and take time to analyse the implications and real benefits of China's policy. After all, China is advancing aggressive superpower ambitions and may in the long-term harden its stance to ensure their achievement. As with the United States, Chinese ambitions and national interests will come first.

China is itself a developing country –
in fact the largest developing country
in the world. It shares with Africa a
similar history of exploitation and
domination by the West.

Concerns have already been raised about Chinese business ethics, which in some cases are allegedly worse than the Western countries. Caution needs to be taken to ensure that China is not another version of an imperialist. Already China is strategically aligning itself to NEPAD, carefully described in its policy as 'an encouraging picture of African rejuvenation and development'. One wonders if this enthusiasm with NEPAD is all about genuine concern for Africa's development or the obvious benefit from the programme's huge infrastructural intentions across Africa.

The excitement around the 'new' Chinese approach creates the perception that China is offering Africa a better aid package – but is this necessarily true? Much like the West, China's development aid to Africa has centred around grants, loans and technical expertise. Currently, the technicalities and dynamics of Chinese aid are not very transparent as the deals are brokered at bilateral (government to government) level.

Technical expertise

Western donors have traditionally made the provision of technical expertise a condition of their development aid. This has come in the form of human resources and the procurement of equipment and machinery. A recent study by Action Aid International revealed that technical aid is one of the major impediments to the effectiveness of development aid. Up to 60 per cent of aid to developing countries is tied to technical expertise – consultants and procuring machinery and spare parts from the donor country. In its current forms, technical aid serves the objectives of the donor country more than the recipient's.

One consequence has been the lack of capacity-building benefit and knowledge transfer to the recipient as locals are blocked from occupying high positions, leading to a dependence on external expertise – and failure to develop a human resource pool.

On technical expertise the Chinese have proved worse than the West. In many cases the Chinese even import Chinese casual labourers, leaving the majority of locals in the cold although Africa has an abundance of unskilled labour which could immensely benefit from these projects. Increased individual income has the potential to lift family standards of living and therefore contribute towards the achievement of MDGs. So far the Chinese are not contributing significantly to this objective.

In post-conflict countries like Sierra Leone, citizens are concerned that Chinese construction and other projects should ideally create employment

---

China chooses to concentrate on the huge infrastructural investments, production and trade, and investments – and less on charity and the social sectors – and the turnover from these have proved more beneficial than development aid.

---

for the hundreds of thousands of restive unemployed youths, who could provide fertile grounds for recruitment by anyone wanting to restart conflict. Chinese aid, and especially technical aid should be adjusted to consider such circumstances. While it should be targeted at reducing unemployment in Africa, it is instead targeted at reducing unemployment in China.

As early as the 1970s, China imported thousands of its own nationals to work as labourers to construct the TAZARA railway. In Angola the construction of a major highway has brought in more than 700 Chinese workers and in Zambia, the Chinese population grew from 300 in 1991 to 3,000 in 2006 as the number of Chinese projects increased. The Chinese seem to bring in more Chinese labourers than required for any project. Inadequate Chinese labour standards have also been reported across Africa, with allegations of overworking, underpaying workers and not adhering to health and safety standards.

Technical aid is thus undoubtedly one of the areas with which Africa will have to battle as Chinese labour does not seem to be a negotiable part of Chinese aid packages. Africa should draw up its own policy on technical aid and labour to ensure that collaboration with China will assist in reducing unemployment.

Trade

Europe has long been Africa's largest trading partner. But Africa-Sino trade is estimated to have grown from US$4 billion in 1995 to US$40 billion in 2005 and is still growing. Trade agreements brokered and forecasts announced at the summit point to US$100 billion by 2010. Africa–Europe trade has significantly reduced from 44 per cent to 32 per cent of Africa's total and the figure will continue to go down.

Such a significant increase in trade is an answer to the region's calls for more trade and reason just enough for Africa to engage more with China – but it must be done strategically. The benefit to Africa in monetary terms should not come at the expense of environmental sustainability and resource depletion. Both China and Africa should develop policies to safeguard environmental and sustainability concerns about the extraction of resources from the continent.

The Beijing consensus

China's aid commitments as stated in the China–Africa policy were further elaborated on during the Sino-Africa summit in November 2006 where the eastern nation pledged to double aid to Africa to US$5 billion for direct investments ($3 billion in preferential loans, $2 billion in export credits) by 2009 and increase the number of loans, development projects in health and agriculture and also the amount of debt cancellation.

The most significant boost will be in the area of human resource development and technical expertise where the continent will benefit from the training of 15,000 Africans, 100 senior Chinese agricultural experts sent to Africa, construction of 60 hospitals and malaria clinics, anti-malaria drugs, 100 new schools and increased scholarships for Africans.

And yet the doubled Chinese aid will come in the form of loans. The conditions attached to these loans are not yet public. Admittedly, the Chinese loans are cheaper than Western ones and come with fewer political and other conditionalilites and penalties than the IFI Poverty Reduction Growth Facility (PRGF). Chinese aid has one major political conditionality attached to it – adherence to the 'One China' policy. Any country engaging China cannot engage Taiwan. The caveats of this conditionality may, however, breed other political conditionalities not yet clear to Africans at this stage.

The Chinese loans also have attached to them economic conditionalities to allow Chinese firms access to Africa resources, the repatriation of profits and the use of their own labour. It is also not yet clear what the implications of these loans will be on the continent's debt crisis. The West has often been accused of double-counting or discounting aid and one cannot help but wonder if the Chinese offer for debt relief, technical assistance, scholar-

---

On technical expertise the Chinese have proved worse than the West. In many cases the Chinese even import Chinese casual labourers, leaving the majority of locals in the cold although Africa has an abundance of unskilled labour which could immensely benefit from these projects.

---

ships and exchange visits will not also be double counted as a part of the aid package. Their formula is not yet known to the majority of the African people and it is therefore a misrepresentation to claim that Chinese aid is free of conditionalities. China should be engaged strategically to minimise any negative impacts of its aid.

So far, grants seem to constitute a small percentage of the Chinese aid – a clear departure from the calls for more grants than loans. Although loans will be acquired on more concessionary terms, these still have to be paid back and have potential to add to the debt crisis. China's debt relief is a partial deal with a cut off date of 2005. It is therefore sensible to conclude that Chinese aid may not be significantly different from Western aid and therefore may not move Africa towards the achievement of the Millennium Development Goals.

Conclusion

Africa's resource gap has often subjected it to exploitation by some 'partners' and yet because of its limited options, the continent has had to bear with these exploitative relationships, subjecting its masses to deeper poverty, humiliation and desperation for the sake of accessing resources. The IFI conditionality regime is a classic example where Africa has had to subject itself to humiliating top–bottom relationships resulting in the IFIs maintaining a perpetual heavy grip on the continent. To date nearly all African countries are still undertaking IFI-imposed structural adjustment programmes off tangent to the interests of their peoples. The result of these programmes has been increased poverty, debt and dependency.

This has made China's seemingly softer approach more attractive. For a change, a policy document approach emphasises a win–win scenario, friendship, mutual benefit and therefore horizontal rather that previous top-bottom Western approaches.

Constant interference in domestic affairs has been a typical feature of Western aid. The West has had to be coerced, by years of lobbying and advocacy, into adopting measures like the Paris Declaration in efforts to tip the scales in favour of the developing world. Even then this agenda has not been fully embraced by all donors as they see themselves losing their autonomy in the process.

The West is keen to criticise China's stance in Africa, branding China as irresponsible and reckless due to its non-interference policy which the West sees as giving African leaders leeway to perpetuate human rights violations. It is, however, doubtful that this criticism is a result of genuine concern for African welfare rather than the jealousy of a competitor.

Yet as both parties potentially have something good to offer Africa, it is only sensible to combine the two. The current competitive approach is not beneficial to Africa and the West should not see China as a threat to its relationship with Africa. It should not see itself as Africa's saviour but as its partner. The 'saviour attitude' is itself a cause of the competition.

Africa should be left alone to choose whom it should engage with as long as it engages in strategic and beneficial relationships. As far as aid is concerned (grants, loans and technical expertise), Chinese aid is not significantly different from Western aid. On its own part, for China to increase the effectiveness of its aid, it should urgently revisit its technical aid agreements, increase grants as opposed to loans, and find a beneficial non-exploitative way of accessing African resources.

Moreblessings Chidaushe is a lobby and advocacy programme officer with the African Forum and Network on Debt and Development (AFRODAD), based in Harare, Zimbabwe. She holds a master's degree in international development from the University of Bath, UK.

CHINA IN AFRICA:
CHALLENGING US GLOBAL HEGEMONY

HORACE CAMPBELL

Africans everywhere are seeking to make the break with the iterations of war and plunder and have instinctively reached out to China. In the long run, writes Horace Campbell, as Africans transform their societies it will be their task to ensure that the relations between Africa and China do not repeat the centuries of underdevelopment and exploitation.

Hence to fight and conquer in all your battles is not supreme excellence; supreme excellence consists in breaking the enemy's resistance without fighting
Sun Tzu

This adage of the Chinese philosopher is today being borne out with the development of the People's Republic of China as a global political and economic force. In the first decade of the 21st century, China has been able to enter political, military and commercial deals with countries of the ASEAN community, Latin America and the countries and observers of the Shanghai Cooperation Organisation (SCO). In November 2006, China sealed this circle with a strategic partnership with Africa through the Forum on China–Africa Cooperation (FOCAC).

Behind the language of friendship and cooperation lay an understanding of the vast treasures of Africa and the major genetic, mineral and energy resources that are coveted in this century of converging technologies. From the dawn of human transformations the resources of Africa attracted friends and invaders. Arab traders had travelled far and wide making links in Africa in the period prior to European colonial penetration. At the end of the

19th century, Bismarck remarked after the Berlin Conference that 'he who controls Africa will control Europe'. Bismarck represented the militarist, masculinist and chauvinist ideas that were to be later associated with the crimes of the imperial partitioning of Africa.

Walter Rodney outlined the imperatives behind imperial Europe in *How Europe Underdeveloped Africa*. Britain and France fought major wars of occupation to control African gold, copper, cocoa and rubber, while a system of apartheid was established to ensure the profitability of European settler farms, factories and mines. At the end of the cold war, inter-imperialist rivalry led to the ascendancy of the US, nudging out the Europeans by embarking on military and commercial partnerships with a number of African states under the guise of supporting growth and development in Africa.

Towards the end of the 20th century, the US established formal agreements

---

*Behind the language of friendship
and cooperation lay an understanding of
the vast treasures of Africa and the major genetic,
mineral and energy resources that are coveted
in this century of converging technologies.*

---

through the Africa Growth and Opportunity Act in order to make direct links with African entrepreneurs. Both the Clinton and Bush administrations had agreed to redefine US relationships with Africa as a 'mutually beneficial partnership based not only on common interests but [also] mutual respect'.

In reality, however, there was never any respect for Africans or real change in the racist policies of the US government.

In response to the US challenge, the European Union established the Development of Partnership for Peace and Security and outlined the 'European Union Strategy for Africa'. The EU committed itself to 'better and faster relations' with Africa based on finance, budgetary support coordination and coherence.

This counter to US competition was especially important for former colonial countries such as Britain, Belgium, Portugal, Germany, and especially France. Both France and Britain had been sufficiently concerned about US encroachment in Africa to induce them to forget their former rivalries.

The emergence of China as a force in Africa complicated the tussle between the EU and US over 'who controls Africa'. The end of the cold war, the end of apartheid and the defeat of Mobutu had speeded up a new approach to unity, leading to the transformation of the OAU into the African Union. The AU set out to chart a course for the political and economic integration of Africa, and systematically sought to re-link Africa with its dispersed diaspora. China aligned itself to the AU and established new areas of cooperation, especially in the rebuilding of the infrastructure of war torn countries such as Angola. It was no accident that Angola was also a major oil exporting country with vast reserves of oil and natural gas. Angola had suffered from the military destabilisation of the US and cold war warriors during the rampage of Jonas Savimbi, yet the same countries that destroyed Angola were making critical commentary on the bold entrance of China into the Angolan economy. Chinese diplomacy provided space for manoeuvre for Africans by laying the basis for an alternative international system in the 21st century.

China had suffered from humiliation and occupation during its colonial period and the demands of the Chinese for transformation and respect is followed very closely on the African continent. The late Abdurrahman Mohammed Babu had been an early advocate of closer relations with China. In his book, *The Future that Works*, Babu had more than two decades ago spelt out the positive benefits of closer relations between China and Africa.[1] Babu had been instrumental in the negotiations with Chou en Lai for the construction of the Tazara railway line to break dependence on Rhodesia. In his analysis and writings, Babu stressed the need for a break with the old colonial model of exporting raw materials. Though Babu was not yet familiar with the impact of *African Fractals: Modern Computing and Indigenous Design* on contemporary mathematical thinking his analysis was using the concept of recursion to conceptualise a new path forward.[2]

Africans everywhere are seeking to make the break with the iterations of war and plunder and have instinctively reached out to China. The new relations between Africa and China could be described in the words of Gramsci, as, 'the old is dying yet the new is yet to be born'. Chinese relations with Africa combine elements of the old (extraction of raw materials), yet the experience of transformation in China ensures that there are many positive and negative lessons to be learnt from China. I argue that, in the short term, one of the most important roles of China will be to assist the break in the disarticulation between the financial sectors and the productive sectors of the economies and to break the outflow of capital from Africa. In the long run the experience of linking new ideas of science and technology to a homegrown path of reconstruction can be an important lesson for Africa. State to state relations are usually opportunistic and it is for this reason that in the long run transnational civil society links between the Chinese peoples and the African peoples will be more important that the relations between leaders.

The historic meeting between the Chinese leaders and representatives of 48 governments in Africa took place in the Chinese capital in November 2006 at the same time that the US was bogged down in the quagmire of Iraq. The massive loss of lives in Iraq and the destruction wrought by US military occupation exposed the new reality of the diminution of America's prestige and credibility. It was in this period that there were major changes in the international system: for example, increased prices for commodities, new centres of financial investments, rapid increase and spread of technology (especially information technology) and the political left turn in Latin America with the election of radical nationalist leaders in Brazil, Bolivia, Ecuador, Venezuela, Nicaragua, Chile, Uruguay and Argentina. The wars in the Middle East and Afghanistan, the lack of response to the ravages of Hurricane Katrina, as well the imperial military posture of the sole super-power, all resulted in a negative image of the US. The distinctive image of Chinese workers laying the foundations for a new communications infrastructure in Angola and Nigeria sharply contrasted with the images of US special forces military personnel deployed to fight terrorism under the Pan Sahel Initiative.

China today is drawing on the long relationships that were developed out of the struggles of the Chinese communist party and the links that were developed during the time of Chairman Mao. It was as if the Chinese leadership wanted to bring home the point that they were opposed to the colonial depictions of Africa in the Western media to the point that the Chinese leader said clearly, 'In the new era, China and Africa share increasing common interests and have a growing mutual need.'

Following the Beijing summit, Western commentators were quick to understand the historic importance of this meeting for Africa. The German chancellor, Angela Merkel, said pointedly: 'We Europeans should not leave the commitment to Africa to the People's Republic of China ... We must take a stand in Africa.'[3]

The most serious worry for the US was expressed by the spokespersons of the International Monetary Fund (IMF) and the World Bank who complained that China's unrestricted lending had 'undermined years of painstaking efforts to arrange conditional debt relief'. They were clearly concerned that China could now offer favourable loans to Africa and, consequently, weaken imperial leverage over African economies. Furthermore,

---

China's trade and economic assistance to Africa has grown by geometric proportions so that by the end of 2006 China will surpass Japan and US in economic assistance to Africa.

---

as a German newspaper expressed it: 'The dollar is still the world's reserve currency, even though it hasn't deserved this status for a long time. The devaluation of the dollar can't be stopped – it can only be deferred. The result could be a world economic crisis.'[4]

The decline of US imperial hegemony has been hastened by the internal contradictions of the social system and the mistaken belief of the US that military power can be substituted for economic strength. Chinese planners and government functionaries understand that the devaluation of the dollar is being deferred by China itself, hence the accelerated plans for investments and forging of alliances across all continents. Chinese planners foresee an era where African minerals and genetic resources will be more worthwhile than US Treasury bills.

China has slowly built up a network of relations through five continents to counter US influence. Despite the drive for the search for raw materials and the traditional forms of current investment, the pace of technological change is occurring so fast that there will be unforeseen consequences for both China and Africa because neither can escape the implications of the qualitative leaps in economic activities that will emanate from the solar revolution and the convergence of new technologies.

China as a global power

China's trade and economic assistance to Africa has grown by geometric proportions so that by the end of 2006 China will surpass Japan and US in economic assistance to Africa. The day after the summit, it was reported that foreign exchange reserves of China had surpassed US$1 trillion. The Chinese State Administration of Foreign Exchange announced that foreign exchange holdings from foreign trade had been expanding at the rate of US$18.8 billion a month during 2006.

At the end of 2000, China's forex reserves stood at US$165.6 billion, but by 2006 the aggressive economic and commercial activities had placed China in a position where it held 20 per cent of the world's foreign exchange with about 70 per cent of its holdings in dollars. In contrast, US debt had risen to over US$8.5 trillion. China is now the fourth largest economy in the world and it controls more than 10 per cent of all world trade. Its huge domestic market with over 1.5 billion citizens insulates the economy from drastic global capitalist cycles of recessions and booms. It was totally impervious to the 1997–98 Asian financial crisis.

The Chinese economy is unusual in that this is a booming capitalist economy controlled by a communist party that is still guided by the dictum of democratic centralism. Essentially socialist in form, but capitalist in content, the forms of industrialisation of the Chinese economy continue to follow the Fordist models long abandoned in the US and Japan.

Chinese auto manufacturers are seeking to surpass the US automobile industry in the next two decades and these developments heighten the concerns of environmentalists who recognise the severe urban air pollution generated by automobiles. Chinese consumption of steel, rubber, glass, oil

The national security strategy
maintained that, 'Our first objective is
to prevent the re-emergence of a new rival
... that poses a threat on the order of that
posed formerly by the Soviet Union.'

and other raw materials has increased the global demand for raw materials and led to increased competition and higher prices. The rapid growth of the Chinese economy grips the imagination of security experts who ponder the global implications of these economic earthquakes. One of the leading investment firms in the US, Goldman Sachs Investment Company, speculated that, by 2030, Brazil, Russia, India and China (the so-called 'BRIC' economies) will eclipse the rich economies of Europe and North America. This is but one example of 'the new being born'.

US national security strategy for managing China

While investment houses and the OECD were speculating on the potentials of the Chinese economy, US military and security officials have been building military bases and alliances in East Asia and Eurasia up to the border with China. In February 2002, the *Washington Post* published a map of the military bases of the USA and the projections of US power in Asia. Following the invasion of Iraq in March 2003, US forward bases expanded in the Middle East and Eurasia, while NATO expanded right up to the border of Russia. US military facilities and cooperative security locations were expanded in the so-called 'fight against terrorism', but in reality this was an excuse for unilateral expansionism. Although the authors who wrote about *Resource Wars* and the *Global Chessboard* explained this expansion on the basis of US petroleum interests in Central Asia, there are other analyses that point to the US forward planning being preparation for dealing with the long term impact of the growth in the Chinese economy. The National Intelligence Council's Global Trends 2015 study, published in 2000, claimed that by 2015 China 'will have deployed tens to several tens of missiles with nuclear warheads targeted against the United States. ... [and] would seek to adjust regional power arrangements to its advantage, risking conflict with neighbours and some powers external to the region'. This document was in essence a muted expression of the old anti-communist position.

The national security strategy paper published by the Bush administration in September 2002 declared that no state will be allowed to challenge the military supremacy of the United States in the 21st century. Inter alia, the National Security strategy maintained that, 'Our first objective is to prevent the re-emergence of a new rival ... that poses a threat of the order of that posed formerly by the Soviet Union. ... Our strategy must now refocus on precluding the emergence of any potential future global competitor.'

Subsequent to the invasion and occupation of Iraq, there were significant military reversals for the US strategy in Afghanistan and Iraq. In light of these reversals, and the clear rifts within the US military establishment, there was another national security strategy position paper presented by the Princeton Project on National Security. This high level review published at the end of September 2006 called for 'managing the relations with China' and urged the US establishment to develop a political and economic strategy to 'engage China'. [5]

The significance of this document lay in the call for a closer alliance between the European Union and the United States in building a 'concert of democracies'. Emphasising that China was a major purchaser of US debt, and acknowledging the limited economic options in relation to the rise of China as a major force in the world economy, the Princeton luminaries returned to the discourse of 'strategic partnership' between China and the US. Despite this retreat from the strident language of the 2002 national security doctrine paper, there was no retreat from the concept of full spectrum dominance that formed the basis of the military planning of the Pentagon.

Chinese long term planning

Chinese leaders studied the plans of the US establishment and set about the process for the projection of multidimensional power along with the building of new alliances. The most important new alliance was its relations with the

European Union (in particular Germany), the countries of Asia, Latin America and the Caribbean, Iran and India and, most importantly, the countries of the Shanghai Cooperation Organisation. A strategic alliance between China and Russia is at the base of the SCO, but it also includes Kazakhstan, Kyrgyzstan, Tajikistan and Uzbekistan. These countries cover an area of over 30 million km^2, or about three-fifths of Eurasia, with a population of 1.455 billion, about a quarter of the world's total. Its working languages are Chinese and Russian. Furthermore, Mongolia, Iran, Pakistan and India have observer status, all of whom – except India – having applied for full membership. With one trillion dollars in reserves and with Russia holding large reserves of foreign currency, the Russian and Chinese leaders have agreed to bilateral financial and trade agreements outside of the sphere of the dollar.

Iran moved to deepen its ties with both Russia and China. At the same time Iran and China signed major energy deals.

In March 2004, China's state-owned oil trading company, the Zhuhai Zhenrong Corporation, signed a 25-year deal to import 110 million tons of liquefied natural gas from Iran. This was followed by a much larger deal between another of China's state-owned oil companies, Sinopec, and Iran, signed in October 2004. This huge deal also enlists substantial Chinese investment in Iranian energy exploration, drilling and production as well as in petrochemical and natural gas infrastructure.

Chinese influence in Asia

The consolidation of Chinese-Russian relations emerged after 20 years of developing similar relationships in East Asia. Driven by the dynamic growth in the Chinese economy, the Asian region bounced back from the economic crisis of 1997. Chinese economic transformation anchored the recovery of the states that had been looted after the Asian crisis, and China replaced Japan as the central economic actor in Asia. Together with Malaysia, Singapore and South Korea, Asian economies had become major players in the world economy. By the end of 2005, they contributed over 33 per cent of world output. China has become a major force in the ASEAN group of nations selectively cooperating with Japan on issues that can lead to regional economic stability.

The massive investments of China in East Asia and the consolidation of a new financial/commercial architecture outside the framework of the Breton Woods institutions has been one of the most outstanding achievements of the Chinese government in the past decade. China is also involved with the countries of East Asia in the setting up of the infrastructure for an Asian Bond Market. One of the goals of this bond market is to mobilise Asian savings for Asian long-term investment in local currencies thus reducing reliance on international capital markets.

The US maintains an expensive and expansive network of military bases across the Asia-Pacific region but the shift in Chinese power has meant that even countries such as Singapore and Malaysia have refused to participate in provocative military exercises in the South China Sea. In the long run it will be the Chinese who will help to decide how the massive military forces of the US Pacific command in the Pacific are paid for.

Two issues – challenging the Breton Woods institutions and raising the question of reparations – endeared the Chinese leaders to Third World leaders, contributing to the expansion of relations between China and Latin America and the Caribbean.

China and Latin America

While developing capitalist enterprises and competing as a global economic power, China still drew on its socialist heritage and anti-imperialist discourse to expand its relations with Latin America and the Caribbean. During 2000–06, China's leaders traversed Latin America, while Latin American politicians visited China to sign new deals. This brand of Third World solidarity coincided with a major political change in Latin America and the Caribbean. Throughout the region, peoples who had suffered from the neoliberal policies of the IMF as well as the exploitative relations that emanated from an oligarchy aligned with the US, used electoral contests to empower new leaders in Venezuela, Bolivia, Brazil, Chile, Argentina, Uruguay, Nicaragua, Peru, and Ecuador. In particular, leaders such as Hugo Chavez of Venezuela and Evo Morales of Bolivia were open in their support for a new path to socialism as well as an alliance with Cuba.

Chinese engagement with Cuba deepened and strengthened the anti-imperialist alliance in Latin America and emboldened the social forces who were seeking alternatives to the crippling effects of the domination of US based multinational corporations. This was the context in which trade deals were signed between China and Brazil, Colombia, Venezuela, Peru, Panama, Ecuador, Chile, Argentina and Uruguay. China has also pledged investments in roads, railways, ports and housing, including assistance for the widening and modernisation of the Panama Canal. China has promised to invest over US$100 billion in the next ten years. China's trade with Latin America has grown from US$200 million in 1975 to over US$40 billion by the end of 2004.

Chinese relations with Africa

It is against this new vibrancy of China in the international arena that one needs to assess the recent China Africa forum in Beijing. Just as China has joined the Caribbean Development Bank (CDB) and participated in new financial instruments in Asia (such as the Asian Bond Market), China has become an energetic member of the African Development Bank. There are plans for the 2007 African Development Bank meetings to be held in China. One of the principal outcomes of the China–Africa summit was the promise of the establishment of a China–Africa development fund. The Chinese president was not shy in drawing attention to the common anti-imperialist struggles of China and Africa. Reminding the leaders of the Sino-Africa solidarity at the height of the Cold War, the Chinese president noted that 2006 marked the 50th anniversary of the inauguration of diplomatic ties between China and African countries.

Despite numerous fine sounding agreements, the relationship between Europe and Africa can be described as neo-colonial. The US and World Bank claim to be fighting poverty in Africa, but after two decades of structural adjustment the conditions of the African poor have worsened, with indices of exploitation and deprivation increasing by geometric proportions. According to one estimate, at the present pace of investment in Africa from the West, it will require more than one hundred years to realise the Millennium Development Goals. Chinese investment potentially provides an alternative for African leaders and entrepreneurs, while providing long term potential for the development of African economies.

There have been criticisms of the Chinese government in their relations with the governments of Sudan and Zimbabwe. China has placed its own energy needs ahead of the needs of people in Sudan, despite the evidence of the genocidal war in Darfur. China has used its position in the UN Security Council to shield the Sudan. It is also clear that the Chinese leadership is making the same errors that were made in the past when it supported Jonas Savimbi in Angola, because Savimbi had presented himself as an enemy of the Soviet Union and Cuba. This episode seems, however, to have been for-

While developing capitalist enterprises and competing as a global economic power, China still drew on its socialist heritage and anti-imperialist discourse to expand its relations with Latin America and the Caribbean.

gotten by the Angolan government which has recently signed major deals with China. The Angolan government has contracted with Chinese companies to repair the infrastructure with contracts worth US$1.9 billion.

Despite the attempt of some to place the stamp of globalisation on these new relations, there are a number of features of Chinese relations with Africa that distinguishes China from the EU and the US. First and most importantly, China was never a participant in the inglorious trans-Atlantic slave trade. Second, there has been no tradition of Chinese colonialism, genocide and occupation in Africa. Third, China embraced the African liberation process with diplomatic, political, material and military support. Fourth, both China and the AU formed the part of the South–South bloc in the World Trade Organisation (WTO), opposing the patenting of life forms and the hegemonistic plans of the US based biotech corporations. Fifth, China has not been identified with the structural adjustment policies that impoverished Africa over the past 30 years. These features must be borne in mind when analysing the medium and long term implications of the Chinese engagement with Africa.

New strategic partnerships with Africa

The Beijing summit witnessed the establishment of a new strategic partnership between China and Africa involving new trade and infrastructural relations with select African countries. An action plan was announced involving Chinese support in areas such as political and economic cooperation, human resource development, culture, education, health, environment, tourism and media. To give meaning to the action plan, a number of initiatives to strengthen this partnership were announced: to double China's 2006 assistance to Africa by 2009; to provide US$3 billion of preferential loans and US$2 billion of preferential buyer's credits to Africa in the next three years; to establish a special fund of US$5 billion to encourage Chinese investment in Africa; and to cancel some debts owed by the heavily indebted poor countries and those least developed countries that have diplomatic ties with China.

In global terms the figures for loans and investments seem minor compared to the kind of investments that China has been making in Asia. But it is the consequent strategic shift in global politics that is significant. The challenge for China is to move beyond declarations and to demonstrate that their relations with Africa will be different in content from the relations and declarations that have been made at the Franco-African summits.

The rapid rise of China is a testament that poor societies can rise beyond colonial exploitation and the mangled priorities of societies that ensure that colonial societies remain a producer of raw materials. Both China and South Korea have demonstrated that poor countries can be transformed through targeted state intervention in the economy. These countries broke with the old models of accumulation and the changes in their economies led to an increased standard of living for their peoples. Thus far China has invested in extraction of minerals and energy in Africa but the inflow of Chinese capital will have a more profound impact especially in relation to the dynamism of the technological revolution, and particularly in Africa's relations with the international financial institutions.

With the rise and dominance of the IMF and World Bank, there has been a massive outflow of capital from Africa. One estimate by Abdulrahaman Babu is that there is about US$200 billion drained from Africa every year associated with structural adjustment programmes of the IMF and the World

Bank. Yash Tandon has drawn attention to the fallacy that foreign direct investment (FDI) has improved the situation, and has shown how FDI has resulted in draining resources out of Africa. This has included remittances of profits, debt payments, loss of capital on account of structural adjustment programmes, privatisation of public assets, patent and copyright fees, management and consultancy fees, biopiracy, and so on.

The dominance of the dollar, pound and the French franc has reinforced the lack of coherence of the African economies. There has been disunity between the financial and economic sectors of the economies. The importance placed on stock exchanges and financial markets (in order to attract investments) has meant that speculators and financial instruments abound in a continent that needs productive capital and trained human resources. Across the continent the stress placed on the development of financial instruments has reinforced the disarticulation of African economies. This disarticulation between the financial sector and the productive sector is most manifest today in Zimbabwe: while its economy has contracted, with inflation running at over 1,000 per cent, Zimbabwe's stock exchange is currently yielding the highest rate of profits in Africa.

This feature of speculative capital dominating African societies is not unique, although Zimbabwe exposes the extreme case of the lack of convergence between financial markets (foreign exchange dealers and speculators)

The rapid rise of China is a testament
that poor societies can rise
beyond colonial exploitation

---

and economic activities; foreign exchange dealers do not service African economies. In Nigeria it is reported that since independence over US$384 billion has been siphoned out of the economy.

Both Nigeria and Zimbabwe are societies where Chinese companies have been active in the past six years. It is not yet clear how the Chinese traders and bankers will deal with this history of speculation and the export of capital. Thus far China does not have the infrastructure of civil society agencies such as non-governmental organisations, missionaries and donor groups to provide the 'humanitarian' cover to smooth the progress of the kind of corruption that is now endemic in Africa. There have been criticisms of Chinese engagement with Africa from workers in the textile sector in both Nigeria and South Africa. It is not by accident that these are societies with very strong trade union and civil society organisations. Domestic civic vigilance may be the best guarantees of preventing the Chinese promise for Africa from turning counter-productive for ordinary people.

Is China a rising imperial state?

This is the question that has been raised by scholars inside and outside of Africa. According to *Pambazuka News*, one of the pre-eminent sites for information on Africa, 'Almost every African country today bears examples of China's emerging presence, from oil fields in the east, to farms in the south, and mines in the centre of the continent. According to a recent Reuters report, Chinese-run farms in Zambia supply the vegetables sold in Lusaka's street markets, and Chinese companies – in addition to launching Nigerian satellites – have a virtual monopoly on the construction business in Botswana.'[6]

These developments have sparked a debate in some quarters on whether China is an imperialist state. If one analyses imperialism as the highest stage of capitalism (in the terms analysed by Lenin at the beginning of the last century), it is not yet possible to characterise the actions of China as imperialist. To grasp the many sided aspects of imperialism it is necessary to revisit both the writings of those such as Lenin and Walter Rodney and the works of Edward Said on culture and imperialism. Western imperialism in Africa is represented by an array of cultural, financial, gendered, religious and military forces. China does not yet have this broad-range presence in Africa. More importantly, after struggling against apartheid and neocolonialism, Africans still have the memory of the kind of organisation necessary to maintain self-determination.

Chinese banks, insurance companies and trading firms do not yet have the kind of self-confidence and track record to act with imperial impunity as the more robust and experienced imperialist entities from those societies that underdeveloped Africa. This is not to say that the capacity for imperial plunder will not arise, but the important point for Africans is that the rise of China is emerging in a period after Africans defeated apartheid and the last vestiges of colonial rule.

Human rights activists point to the relations between China and Sudan and Zimbabwe as examples of the willingness of the Chinese to prop up unpopular leaders. Yet in these societies there are opposition forces that are mobilising to effect change. The present Chinese entry into Africa will be affected by the rise of African social movements and it will be the task of the social movements in Africa to make links with Chinese civil society to expose the realities of the genocidal actions of the Sudanese government (especially in Darfur). Thus far China has been able to escape the quagmire of the politics of the Middle East and has been supportive of those fighting for self-determination in Palestine. It will be the task of the Sudanese and African activists to educate those Chinese who want to understand Africa.

To quote *Pambazuka News* recently: 'It would be wrong to suggest that China's impact only raises problems, or is merely a re-run of past imperialisms. ... But that does not mean that the "Chinese option" could not also be exploited to widen the room for all African states, not only those abusing human rights.'[7]

African peoples and governments are not passive bystanders in the global struggles for a multipolar world. It is in this emerging reality of the struggles for African reconstruction and transformation that the differences between China and Europe lie.

Conclusion

The insertion of Chinese financial resources into Africa is occurring at a moment when there are major technological changes in the world economy. The present thirst for African oil is now driving China but technical change is so rapid that within a generation there will be new sources of energy and new technologies to tap into, both solar energy and hydrogen fuel cell technology. Nano technology, biotechnology, information technology and cognitive technologies are slowly changing the nature of economic relations. In the past ten years the impact of the internet and the cell phone has been felt in the most remote areas of Africa. China is investing in these new technologies. According to *The Guardian* 'the Sahara desert is a vast source of energy that can promise a carbon-free, nuclear-free electrical future for all Europe, if not the world'. The German scientists who made this commentary noted that 'covering just 0.5% of the world's hot deserts with a technology called concentrated solar power would provide the world's entire electricity needs, with desalinated water for desert regions as a valuable by-product, as well as air-conditioning for nearby cities'.

China's economy is growing at a pace where it will need to keep abreast of these technical changes. Chinese and Indian universities are now competing with North American and European universities in many profound ways. The new partnership between China and Africa opens new opportu-

The insertion of Chinese financial resources into Africa is occurring at a moment when there are major technological changes in the world economy

nities for African intellectuals and activists who want to move Africa in a new direction. People to people relations between the Chinese and African peoples can lay the foundations for exchanges between African and Chinese traditional healers, between African and Chinese health workers and between Chinese and African engineers and scientists. China has been able to transform its economy while retaining those aspects of Chinese knowledge system that emanated from the long history of Chinese society. This is one area where the interest of Africans and the Chinese converge.

The other area where their interests converge is on reparations. China has been forthright in its call for the Japanese to rewrite its textbooks to reflect a different account of the Japanese occupation of China. African activists share the same goal of calling on Europe and the US to repair their relations with Africa after centuries of the slave trade and colonialism. After the end of colonialism and apartheid, European societies continue to teach their children that Europe entered Africa in order to civilise the savages.

This discourse reproduces the culture of imperialism and continues with the international non-governmental organisations representing the modern missionaries in Africa.

We started this analysis by quoting the Chinese philosopher Sun Tzu on the question of breaking the resistance of the enemy without fighting. In this analysis I have argued that in less than a decade the decline of the US has accelerated and the Chinese have been able to break out of US military encirclement without engaging the US militarily. At the same time the opening for socialism in Latin America and the investment of the Chinese opened new opportunities for alternative modes of economic organisation. Since the start of the war in Iraq this process has accelerated. These changes have affected Africa in a profound way. Most profound of all is the ability of Africans to defy the conditionalities of the Bretton Woods institutions. This defiance will have an impact on the dollar as the currency of world trade.

China is seeking to diversify its holdings away from the dollar, and investment in Africa in the long run will prove more profitable than holding dollars. It is this reality that ensures that the role of China in Africa will intensify in the short run. At the meeting of the African Union in July 2006, Hugo Chavez, the President of Venezuela called for the establishment of a Bank of the South to replace the World Bank. African scholars who have been critical of the submissive ideas behind NEPAD can study the implications of the 'dollar illusion' for Africa and work with other societies that have been colonised to establish the 'International Bank for Reparations and Reconstruction'.

In the long run as Africans transform their societies it will be their task to ensure that the relations between Africa and China do not repeat the centuries of underdevelopment and exploitation. While this new road is being built, African peace activists will have to work with the international peace movement to ensure that the old competition of capitalism does not lead to another global war.

Horace G. Campbell is professor of African American studies and political science at Syracuse University in Syracuse, New York. He is the author of Reclaiming Zimbabwe: The Exhaustion of the Patriarchal Model of Liberation.

Notes

1 Salma Babu and Amrit Wilson (2002) *The Future that Works: Selected Writings of A. A. Babu.* Trenton: Africa World Press.

2 Ron Eglash (1999) *African Fractals: Modern Computing and Indigenous Design.* New Jersey: Rutgers University Press.

3 Jilio Godoy (2006) 'China Swaggers into Europe's Backyard', *Asia Times*, 17 November <http://www.atimes.com/atimes/China_Business/HK17Cb03.html>.

4 Gabor Steingart (2006) 'America and the Dollar Illusion', Der *Spiegel* 25 October. See also Gabor Steingart (2006) *World War for Wealth: The Global Grab for Power and Prosperity.* Munich: Piper Verlag.

5 G. John Ikenberry and Anne-Marie Slaughter (Princeton Project on National Security) (2006) *Forging a World of Liberty under Law: US National Security in the 21st Century.* Princeton: The Woodrow Wilson School of Public and International Affairs, Princeton University <http://www.wws.princeton.edu/ppns/report/FinalReport.pdf>.

6 Stephen Marks (2006) 'China in Africa – The New imperialism?', *Pambazuka News* < http://www.pambazuka.org/en/category/features/32432>

7 Stephen Marks (2006).

ENVIRONMENTAL IMPACT:
MORE OF THE SAME?

MICHELLE CHAN-FISHEL

Is China friend or foe to the African continent? Michelle Chan-Fishel writes that while China's investments do involve socio-economic development, environmental and social problems are emerging 'with a new face'. Chan-Fishel looks at Chinese interests in Sudan, Angola, Nigeria, Zambia, Zimbabwe, Democratic Republic of Congo, Gabon, Equatorial Guinea, Cameroon and Liberia. 'Chinese companies are quickly generating the same kinds of environmental damage and community opposition that Western companies have spawned around the world.'

Introduction

For many African governments, China's emergence from poverty to becoming an economic powerhouse serves as an inspirational example. From the mid-1980s, China's pursuit of market economics, with a focus on export-oriented industrialisation and inward foreign direct investment, helped raise GDP and build infrastructure. In many parts of Africa, China is perceived by governments as an 'economic messiah', a new investor and ally in a world where there is growing unease over what African governments perceive to be the patronising attitudes of the West.

The president of the African Development Bank Donald Kaberuka has remarked: 'We can learn from them (China) how to organize our trade policy, to move from low- to middle-income status, to educate our children in skills and areas that pay off in just a couple of years.'[1] Similarly, Mozambican President Armando Emilio Guebuza has said: 'When we see China coming up and developing an attitude of support to help our productivity, we

Africans say "Welcome", because these investments and projects, especially in infrastructure, will help reduce our poverty problems.'[2]

There are currently an estimated 750 Chinese companies operating in 50 African countries. But Beijing's African investments are also tied to socio-economic development, including debt relief, grants, soft loans, buyer credits provided by state-owned banks, scholarships, preferential market access, and technical aid in the fields of medicine, agriculture and engineering.

Concerns

The economic foundation of China's relationship with Africa is obvious: the procurement of natural resources. Beijing's only political condition for establishing ties between China and African countries is the 'one China principle' – refusal to diplomatically recognise Taiwan.

But China's no-strings-attached support has sounded alarm bells in the West. Recently, World Bank president Paul Wolfowitz criticised Beijing for undercutting anti-corruption measures, such as requiring revenue transparency for resource extraction projects. Some human rights watchdogs have notably criticised China for weakening democracy and human rights in Africa through its readiness to deal with – and sometimes sell arms to – the Sudanese, Angolan and Zimbabwean governments.

Accusations of 'neo-colonialism' have already surfaced, as China's search for energy and minerals is reminiscent of the 'scramble for resources' that characterised Western colonialism. The history of natural resource extraction in Africa has a poor track record, characterised by environmental degradation and increased poverty. As Chinese companies become increasingly involved in the oil and gas, mining, and logging sectors, these environmental and social problems are emerging with a new face.

Oil and gas

To help fuel its booming economy, China is investing in Africa's oil rich countries like never before. Since the late 1990s, China has invested billions in Sudan, Angola, and Nigeria to secure drilling rights. Africa has become a key oil exporter to China: in 2005 China imported about 700,000 barrels per day of oil from the continent, approximately 30 per cent of its total oil imports. China anticipates increasing that amount by 25 per cent in the next 10 years, and has been carefully paving the way to ensure its objective is met.[3]

Sudan

Perhaps the most controversial of China's oil interests, and one that demonstrates well China's commitment to secure oil deals is its relationship with Sudan.[4] Beijing is the leading developer of oil reserves in the Sudan,[5] currently importing 60 per cent of the country's oil output.[6] Today, the China National Petroleum Corporation (CNPC) is the largest shareholder in the Greater Nile Petroleum Operating Company (GNPOC). What makes China's involvement in Sudan so controversial are the atrocities occurring in

---

Mozambican President Armando Emilio Guebuza has said: 'When we see China coming, we Africans say "Welcome", because these investments and projects, especially in infrastructure, will help reduce our poverty problems.'

---

the western region of Darfur, atrocities which the US and other nations have branded genocide. Numerous human rights groups have accused Sudan of systematically massacring civilians and chasing them from ancestral lands to clear oil-producing areas.

Prior to the conflict in Darfur, China was suspected of financially underwriting Sudan's 21-year civil war, which ended with the signing of a permanent peace accord in January 2005. In 2000, Sudanese resistance forces were said to be collecting photographs of Chinese-made weapons to prove the increase in Beijing's support for Khartoum. In July 2000, *WorldNetDaily* reported that Sudan had acquired 34 new jet fighters from China.[7] In June 2001, the *Mideast Newsline* reported that Sudan had built three weapons factories with Chinese assistance in order to halt rebel advances.[8] China also reportedly provided arms support to Sudan in exchange for oil.[9] Although it is difficult to determine exactly how much money China has invested in Sudan, one source states that 'China reportedly invested US$20 billion in Sudan, apart from soft loans, grants and other forms of aid.'[10] According to a study by PFC Strategic Studies, the Sudanese government could collect as much as US$30 billion or more in total oil revenue by 2012.[11]

Angola

In recent years, Angola[12] has emerged as one of China's top trading partners. Last year, China was busy securing long-term oil agreements with Angola, and Sonangol (Angola's state-run petroleum company) committed to provide long-term oil supplies to China's Sinopec. Sonangol and Sinopec will evaluate Angola's offshore Block 3, and will also jointly study plans for a new oil refinery.[13] In October 2004, as India was preparing to close a major deal for about US$620 million to buy Shell's 50 per cent share in Block 18, China made a last minute bid – to win the deal. China's offer of US$2billion in aid for various projects in Angola made India's offer of US$200 million for developing railways pale in comparison.[14]

   In post-conflict Angola, human rights problems are still prevalent in oil-producing areas of the country. For example, Human Rights Watch reports that:

> Since late 2002, some 30,000 Angolan troops have been deployed in Cabinda, a discontiguous province that produces around 60 percent of the country's oil revenue... the Angolan army arbitrarily detained and tortured civilians with impunity in Cabinda, and continue to restrict their freedom of movement despite an apparent end to the decades-long separatist conflict.[15]

Nigeria

Previously, China had been shut out of Nigeria[16] by Western firms. However, through patience, political prowess and technological contributions, such as promising to build and launch a communication satellite for Nigeria by 2007, Chinese firms are gaining a foothold in the industry. In December 2004, China's Sinopec and Nigeria's NNPC signed an agreement to develop oil mining leases 64 and 66, located in the waters of the Niger Delta in southern Nigeria. In July 2005, China's CNOOC signed a contract with NNPC worth US$800 million to guarantee China receives 30,000 barrels per day for one year. Recently, China and Nigeria signed a deal in which China would provide a US$4 billion infrastructure investment package in exchange for first refusal rights on four oil blocks. In time, it is suspected that China could easily replace some of these Western firms when their drilling licences come up for renewal.

The oil trouble in Nigeria is well known, and largely rooted in regional instability and violent conflicts between the government and local militant groups. The best known of these groups is the Movement for the

---

China's search for energy and minerals
is reminiscent of the 'scramble for resources'
that characterised Western colonialism

Emancipation of the Nigerian Delta (MEND), which has demanded more benefits sharing in the oil-producing Niger Delta area. MEND has warned foreign oil firms, including Chinese companies, to stay well clear of the oil producing Niger delta or risk attack.[17] Previously, they attacked facilities belonging to Shell, Nigeria's largest oil producer, in operations that coincided with hostage-taking.[18] The threat to Chinese companies and employees came just days after China signed the US$4 billion infrastructure deal for the refusal rights on four oil blocks.

Mining

China is the world's fastest-growing market for minerals. Africa figures heavily in Beijing's strategies to secure access to mineral resources.

Copper in Zambia

Copper is Zambia's leading export commodity, and production is soaring. The Chamber of Mines forecasts production of about 550,000 tonnes in 2005 and more than 600,000 tonnes in 2006. But as miners try to extract more and more copper ore, the accident rate is soaring. According to the Mineworkers Union of Zambia, at least 71 people died in Zambian mining accidents in 2005.[19] 'We're worried about the accident trends', said Mavuto Gondwe, a union director with responsibility for health and safety.[20] Indeed, in 2005, an explosion at a BGRIMM mine was the biggest single accident in the history of the Zambian mining industry. BGRIMM is controlled and 60 per cent owned by China Non Ferrous Metal Industries, a Chinese government-owned company.

The bubbling resentment against China's unsafe mines and the proliferation of cheap Chinese imports manifested itself in Zambia's September 2006 presidential elections. Leading opposition candidate Michael Sata campaigned on a platform of ejecting Chinese investors, and accused Beijing of vote tampering via Chinese-made computers. His comments in turn prompted Zambia's Chinese ambassador Li Baodong to imply that Beijing might withdraw its investments if Sata prevailed.[21] The candidate only received 29 per cent of the vote, but support for Sata was high in some areas; after the elections riots broke out in which Chinese-owned businesses were attacked.[22]

Coal and platinum in Zimbabwe

Shunned by Western leaders and investors for the government's human rights practices, Zimbabwe has begun a determined campaign to hitch its plummeting fortunes to China's rising star. Zimbabwe's President Mugabe calls the policy 'Look East', and it has resulted in tremendous growth in trade and economic cooperation between the two countries. Several joint venture companies are being established, and under the Zimbabwe-China Joint Commission, Zimbabwe has benefited through the Chinese government's concessionary and interest free loans and grants.[23]

The Chinese are widely reported to covet a stake in Zimbabwe's platinum mines, which have the world's second largest reserves, and the Mugabe government has hinted that it will accommodate them. The mines' principal operator denies being pressured into dealing with the Chinese, but negotiations are under way to sell a stake to Zimbabweans yet to be identified. The operator has postponed major spending on the mines, citing the cause as political uncertainty.[24]

Cobalt in Congo

According to the Cobalt Development Institute (CDI), China was the world's leading cobalt producer in 2005. Approximately three-quarters of all cobalt made in China in that year derived from imported concentrates, of which almost 90 per cent came from the DRC.[25]

While the DRC is making slow progress in its transition process after a four-year civil war, the major regional and international mining houses are anticipating stability in the country.[26] In the Katanga area, Chinese companies such as Colec and Feza Mining are initiating copper and cobalt mining and processing projects.[27] Earlier this year, Nanjing Hanrui Cobalt Co Ltd, one of the largest conglomerates in China, purchased three high-grade copper-cobalt mines in Lubumbashi in the DRC.[28] After a decade of growth, this private company has become the leading cobalt powder producer in Asia, ranking among the top three in the world. Because of the firm's expansion, the international monopoly on cobalt has been broken, and the global cobalt powder prices have been reduced by half. International companies such as Japan's Mitsubishi, Hitachi, Toshiba, Sumitomo, South Korea's Samsung and LG all buy cobalt powder from Nanjing.[29]

Timber[30]

China is the largest importer of forest products in the world, and its imports of forest products have tripled in less than a decade.[31] In 1998, China placed stringent restrictions on domestic logging, forcing the country to import a high percentage of its total wood consumption. Since then, China climbed six spots to become the world's top forest products importer, taking 120,000,000m² in 2004.[32] China is now the leading importer of round logs. In 2003, China was second in industrial roundwood imports, second for wood-based panels, pulp, paper and paper boards, and fifth for sawn wood.[33] China imports 40 per cent of its total forest consumption.[34]

Gabon

Today, China is Gabon's largest timber trading partner.[35] In 2003 Gabon supplied 40 per cent of China's log imports from the west/central Africa region,[36] and China imported 46 per cent of Gabon's total forest exports.[37] Gabonese law requires processing before export, yet China's demands are for raw logs. According to some analysts, China's influence in the sector encourages 'flagrant disregard for the law', and taxes are not paid on 60 per cent of the area allocated as forest concessions.[38] National law states that failure to gain ministry approval of a management plan for a forest concession within three years triggers forfeiture of the concession; yet only five of more than 200 companies (representing 30 per cent of concessions) in 2000 had even stated their intention to start writing a plan. Additionally, all five of these companies had already logged their concessions for more than three years.[39] The illegal timber exports to China have been estimated to be as high as 70 per cent of total timber exports.[40]

Equatorial Guinea

China purchases an estimated 60 per cent of the timber exported from Equatorial Guinea, another country with known illegal logging problems. According to the World Wildlife Fund, annual timber extraction in Equatorial Guinea exceeds the maximum legally allowed limit by 40–60 per cent.[41] It is also estimated that up to 90 per cent of the total harvest going to China is illegal.[42] Shimmer International, a subsidiary of the notorious Rimbunan Hijau, has close ties with the minister of forests. Along with its many subsidiaries and associated companies, it is the dominant player in the country's logging sector.[43] China's Jilin Forest Industry (Group) is also involved in timber extraction and processing.[44]

Cameroon

Cameroon exports about 11 per cent of its timber to China.[45] The Centre pour l'Environnement et développement estimates that at least 50 per cent of logging is illegal in Cameroon.[46] According to Friends of the Earth, 96 per cent of logging violations in Cameroon between 1992 and 1993 were followed by incomplete judicial procedures, and one in five cases in this time period were dropped after intervention by an 'influential person'.[47]

Hong Kong-owned Vicwood Pacific acquired the Cameroon subsidiaries of the Thanry Group in 1997. From 2002, Thanry has been one of the principle loggers and international timber traders in the Congo River Basin and had

---

This low-price development model
actually comes at a very high cost – to societies,
both inside and outside China, as well as
to the environment

---

established itself as a major violator of forestry laws and a creator of regional social unrest. Between 2000 and 2002, Thanry was fined over US$1.3 million for what has been called 'anarchic logging', including cutting undersized trees, logging outside legal boundaries, and logging in unallocated concessions.[48] The World Bank also discovered that the origin of many of Thanry's logs had been falsified so as to avoid Cameroon's export controls.[49]

Liberia

In Liberia, rebel leader-turned-president, Charles Taylor relied heavily on timber resources to support his own military efforts and to fund mercenaries in neighbouring Sierra Leone and Côte d'Ivoire. Taylor used the revenue gained from the sale of the timber to buy arms for troops, support foreign mercenaries, create enormous personal wealth, and support the personal security forces that were essential to his power. The timber transport vessels were also used to traffic arms throughout the region.[50]

China has rapidly increased its log imports from Liberia. By 2001, it was Liberia's largest buyer of wood products. That year, China imported US$42 million worth of logs (58 per cent of the country's total exports),[51] most of which came from the OTC through Chinese importer Global Star Tradings.[52] A report commissioned by USAID stated: 'Harvested timber is transported to Liberian ports where it is bartered to Chinese and other trading partners either directly in exchange for weapons and munitions needed by Taylor to carry on his wars, or is sold to raise funds to achieve the same end.'[53] On 6 May 2003, the UN Security Council imposed an embargo on Liberian timber products. China had imported 365,000m³ of logs from Liberia in 2003 before the sanctions. But log imports plunged to 30,000m³ in the second half of 2003; and China did not appear to have imported Liberian logs during the first half of 2004.[54]

Conclusion

While conventional wisdom posits that Chinese multinationals treat their workers and the environment more poorly than their Western counterparts, not enough research has been done to actually prove this hypothesis. What is clear, however, is that Chinese companies are quickly generating the same kinds of environmental damage and community opposition that Western companies have spawned around the world.

For communities adversely affected by these mega-projects (regardless of the corporate sponsor), the question is: first, do they give their free, prior and informed consent to the investment? If the answer is 'yes' then the

ultimately, it will be important to realise
that this low-price/high-cost economic model
will not work: not for Africa, nor for China, nor
for the rest of the world

challenge becomes, 'How can communities and governments negotiate with the sponsor to receive the best deal possible, in terms of economic benefits sharing, human rights, sustained livelihoods, environmental quality, and cultural and community integrity?'

Evaluated this way it is evident that in some cases, what private companies can provide through 'corporate social responsibility' – e.g. health clinics that may or may not be furnished with medicines, books for local schools – pales in comparison with the deals that Chinese state-owned companies can offer (e.g. debt relief, concessional lending).

Furthermore, African leaders and policy makers are faced with additional question when it comes to Chinese investment: Is the Chinese model of development, which admittedly has been characterised by spectacular economic growth, worth emulating? Based on the unlimited extraction of natural resources, ultra low-wage manufacturing, and the export of cheap goods (due especially to 'throwaway' societies in the West), this paradigm

– which is in essence one of corporate globalisation, not of China alone – is simply not sustainable.

This low-price development model actually comes at a very high cost – to societies, both inside and outside China, as well as to the environment. The untold story of China's rapid economic growth is one characterised by vast levels of income disparity, unfair treatment of workers and lost livelihoods, especially in the rural areas. These problems are so acute that they threaten political stability. Environmental problems are similarly acute: breathing the air in China's most polluted cities is the equivalent of smoking two packets of cigarettes a day. On an international level, meanwhile, the effects of corporate globalisation (particularly Western consumption) are leading to the destruction of the ecological support systems on which all life depends.

It is tempting for African leaders to simply want to play Western and Chinese extraction companies off against each other in an effort to 'get a better deal', and doggedly follow China's path of economic growth. Indeed, it is important for them to carefully conceive extraction projects in order to secure the best possible deal for their people. But ultimately, it will be important to realise that this low-price/high-cost economic model will not work: not for Africa, nor for China, nor for the rest of the world.

Michelle Chan-Fishel is programme manager of Friends of the Earth's green instruments project.

Notes

1 Moin Siddiqi (2006), 'The Sino-Africa Courtship Continues: New Challenges and Opportunities'. *African Review of Business and Technology.*

2 Moin Siddiqi (2006).

3 'Beijing Wants More African Oil', *Asia News Agencies.*

4 Cindy Hurst 'China's Oil Rush in Africa' . The Institute for the Analysis of Global Security <http://www.iags.org/chinainafrica.pdf>.

5 'China Concludes Oil, Gas Agreement with Algeria', *World Tribune*, 9 February (2004).

6 Jane's Sentinel Security Assessment.

7 Charles Smith (2000), 'Sudan War Heating Up: Clinton Ignores African Atrocities as China Escalates Aid to Khartoum', WorldNetDaily.com, 29 August.

8 'Sudan Builds New Weapons Factories with Chinese Help', *Mideast Newsline*, 17 June 2001.

9 Charles Smith (2000).

10 Happymon Jacob (2004), 'India-Sudan Energy Ties: Implications', Observer Research Foundation (India), 31 August.

11 Peter Goodman (2004), 'China Invests Heavily in Sudan's Oil Industry', *Washington Post*, 23 December.

12 Cindy Hurst.

13 *Afrol News* (2005) 'China, Angola Sign 9 Cooperation Agreement', 7 March.

14 Human Rights Watch (2004) 'China Beats India for Angola Oil Deal', CRI Online, 19 October.

15 Human Rights Watch (2004) 'Angola: In Oil-Rich Cabina, Army Abuses Civilians', 23 December <http://hrw.org/english/docs/2004/12/23/angola9922.htm>.

16 Cindy Hurst.

17 Dino Mahtani (2006) 'Stay Away from Delta, Nigerian Rebels Tell China', *Financial Times*, 1 May.

18 Ibid.

19 Jackie Range (2005) 'Zambia's Miners Pay High Price for Copper Boom', Dow Jones Newswires, 12 October <http://www.minesandcommunities.org/Action/press791.htm>.

20 Ibid.

21 Robyn Dickson (2006) 'Africans Lash Out at Chinese Employers', *Los Angeles Times*, 6 October.

22 David Blair (2006) 'Rioters Attack Chinese After Zambian Poll', *The Daily Telegraph*, 3 October.

23 *Africa News* (2006) 'Zimbabwe: Sino-Africa Relations Beneficial', 6 April.

24 Michael Wines (2005) 'From Shoes to Aircraft to Investment, Zimbabwe Pursues a Made-in-China Future', *The New York Times*, 24 July.

25 RIA OREANDA (2006) 'China Becomes World Leader in Production of Cobalt', 28 March.

26 No evidence has yet been found to indicate that cobalt revenues helped finance the civil war. It appears that China and international investors came to the DRC for cobalt after the civil war, when the country had stabilised enough for significant foreign investments.

27 *Africa News* (2005) 'Big Mining Companies Anticipate Growing Stability', 29 September.

28 China Construction Project Net (2006) 'Nanjing Hanrui Cobalt Purchases Three Overseas Copper-Cobalt Mines', 13 April <www.SinoCast.com>

29 Ibid.

30 (2005) 'Chinese Involvement in African Illegal Logging and Timber Trade', testimony of Allan Thornton, President for the Environmental Investigation Agency at the US House of

Representatives, Committee of International Relations, 28 July <http://wwwa.house.gov/international_relations/109/tho072805.pdf>.

31 Forest Trends, 2005 'China's Forest Product Exports: Overview of Trends by Segment and Destinations', (draft publication).

32 Ibid.

33 Sun, Wang and Gu (2005) 'A Brief Overview of China's Timber Market', Forest Trends, January.

34 National Timber Distribution Association (2004) 'China Timber Information', Issue 4.

35 International Tropical Timber Organisation (2004) 'Annual Review and Assessment of the World Timber Situation', Document GI-7/04.

36 Seneca Creek Associates, LLC and Wood Resources International (2004), 'Illegal Logging and Global Wood Markets', LLC, Prepared for AF & PA, November, p.133.

37 Toyne, O'Brien and Nelson (2003) 'The Timber Footprint of the G8 and China: Making the Case for Green Procurement by Government',"WWF International, June, p. 31.

38 James Hewitt (2002) 'China: Illegal Imports and Exports', Global Timer, July.

39 Global Forest Watch, World Resources Institute (2002) 'A First Look at Logging in Gabon'.

40 James Hewitt (2002).

41 Paul Toyne, Cliona O'Brian and Rod Nelson (2002), 'The Timber Footprint of the G8 and China: Making the Case for Green Procurement by Government', WWF International, June <http://assets.panda.org/downloads/G8_meeting_June2002.pdf>.

42 James Hewitt (2002).

43 Greenpeace (2004) 'The Untouchables: Rimbunan Hijau's World of Forest Crime and Political Patronage', January, p. 11.

44 China Foreign Ministry (2006) 'Equatorial Guinea', 10 October, <http://www.china.org.cn/english/features/focac/183538.htm>

45 Toyne, O'Brian and Nelson (2002).

46 Ed Matthew (2001) 'Briefing: European League Table of Imports of Illegal Tropical Timber', Friends of the Earth, August.

47 Ibid.

48 Greenpeace (2002) 'Vicwood-Thanry: Destroying Cameroon's Ancient Forests', April.

49 World Bank Group (2000) 'Internal Report', October, pp.14–29.

50 Global Witness <www.globalwitness.org/campaigns/forests/liberia>.

51 Global Witness (2002) 'Logging Off: How the Liberian Timber Industry Fuels Liberia's Humanitarian Disaster and Threatens Sierra Leone', September.

52 Global Witness (2004) 'Liberia: Back to the Future', Global Witness Publishing Inc, May.

53 Baker, Murl et al. (2004) 'Conflict Timber: Dimensions of the Problem in Asia and Africa', *Africa Cases*, Vol. 3, reported by ARD, Inc, submitted to USAID.

54 Seneca Creek Associates, LLC and Wood Resources International (2004).

AS THE BEGINNING ENDS: CHINA'S RETURN TO AFRICA

DANIEL LARGE

China-Africa relations received unprecedented attention during 2006, both in terms of visibility and attention, writes Daniel Large. China's involvement is important to consider, he says, because China will continue to need African resources, because of the increased trade and investment in Africa as a result of the relationship and because of an emerging Chinese development agenda on the continent. Unlike early Chinese explorers dating back to 1433, the current Chinese involvement in Africa is here to stay.

China's Year of Africa in 2006 climaxed with the Forum on China-Africa Cooperation (*Zhong Fei Luntan*, or FOCAC). A friend aptly remarked, 'Africa has taken over Beijing!' Beijing mobilised to deliver high standards of Chinese hospitality and red-carpet treatment for 48 African delegations made up of political leaders, businessmen and accompanying journalists. A triangular billboard on Tiananmen Square prominently displayed the China-Africa Forum logo, its vivid green projections of Africa and China foregrounded and the rest of the world painted out in blue. Throughout the city, banners, billboards, posters, and other public spaces, including the metro, restaurants, and shopping areas such as Wanfujing, proclaimed 'Welcome to Beijing Summit' and 'Friendship, Peace, Cooperation and Development' (*youyi, heping, hezuo, fazhan*). Even the Temple of Heaven had large billboards conveying 'Congratulations on the Opening of Beijing Summit'. After extensive media attention prior to the forum, and amidst intensive media coverage of its proceedings, Beijing was also talking Africa. Chinese students explained how China needed resources from Africa, and how China can help Africa.

As the third ministerial and first heads of state conference, this FOCAC, between the 4–5 November 2006, was the most prominent such summit meeting after the first (Beijing, 2000) and the second (Addis Ababa, 2003). In many ways the first FOCAC was a trial run for this more lavish, ambitious and successful summit.[1] It was carefully planned and impressively executed political theatre. Unlike six years ago, not just African but the world media was there to report. The FOCAC was a distinctively bilateral affair, contrasting with the more multilateral celebration of the 50th anniversary of the Bandung conference last year. Its staged choreography, including President Hu Jintao's reception of individual Africa leaders in the Great Hall of the People, resonated with historical overtones of tribute, a contemporary version of 'distant people' arriving in 'uninterrupted succession'.[2] The extensive symbolic, monetary and political capital invested in FOCAC, its near flawless public execution and modern Beijing spoke of an increasingly self-

---

*The forum formally marked the end
of the beginning of China's latest engagement
with Africa, a process qualitatively different from
the past and set to have potentially significant
consequences for Africa.*

---

confident China. Coming at the end of a year which has seen the dramatic irruption of China in Africa as a world media issue, topic of conversation and policy concern for governments, international organisations and civil society groups, it additionally, and very publicly, amounted to a declaration of arrival and positive intent: the Chinese government is serious about developing its African relations, and sought not merely to impress this upon its Africa guests but also the world at large. This forum cemented the official apparatus of cooperation and consolidated the foundations of development. Altogether, it formally marked the end of the beginning of China's latest engagement with Africa,[3] a process qualitatively different from the past and set to have potentially significant consequences for Africa.

This article briefly reflects on the current juncture of China-Africa relations at the end of an eventful 2006. After pointing to what is different about China's return under new circumstances to Africa, it addresses key dynamics of current relations before identifying issues that are likely to increasingly come to the fore as the normalisation of relations proceeds and the exceptionalism that China still enjoys in its African relations wears off.

China's return to Africa

Overall, 2006 was a watershed year for China-Africa relations in terms of the visibility of the subject and attention devoted to it. It featured a number of notable events, starting with the now traditional tour by Chinese Foreign Minister Li Zhaoxing (this time to Cape Verde, Liberia, Mali, Senegal, Nigeria and Libya) and the release of China's Africa policy statement in January. After visiting the United States, President Hu Jintao toured Morocco, Nigeria and Kenya in April, followed by Premier Wen Jiabao's June trip to Egypt, Ghana, the Democratic Republic of Congo, Angola, South Africa, Tanzania and Uganda in June. Besides FOCAC, the wide geographical extent of these high-level tours was reinforced by regional meetings. The second ministerial meeting of the Macau Forum[4] on September 24–25 in Macau featured high-level representation from Angola, Mozambique, Cape Verde, Guinea Bissau, East Timor, Brazil, Macau and China. The Conference of Sino-Arab Friendship, held in Khartoum at the end of November, established a permanent secretariat there under Arab League sponsorship and made a commitment to hold meetings every two years. China has arrived in Africa.

Rather than a sudden explosion into Africa, the Chinese engagement represents a return to the continent in a number of different ways. Strictly speaking, unlike 1433 when the Chinese sea voyages to Africa stopped, China never left Africa in the post-colonial period. The 1980s saw Africa downgraded in China's foreign relations and China's involvement in Africa was gradually reoriented into more commercial forms. Current relations should be traced to China's renewed interest in Africa that was sparked in 1989 and consolidated with Jiang Zemin's tour to six African countries in May 1996, a process that paved the way for the acceleration of the current phase after 2000. Besides the longer history of contact between China and

Africa, the FOCAC occurred on the 50th anniversary of China's establishment of diplomatic relations with Egypt (then the UAR), and was underpinned by a historical foundation emphasising the commonalities China and Africa enjoy: cradles of civilisation, victims of colonialism, a developing country and developing continent.

History imbues the language and approach of China–Africa relations. The use of an interpreted shared past, seen in ritualistic symbolic and instrumental forms, is one salient facet of China's officially mobilised version of its historical connections with Africa, the flip-side of which often comes in the form of virtuous commitments against any future hegemonic role for China in Africa. The historical lineages to the current debate are worth recalling. Debate about the role China can play in African development is not new. In fact, it presents a historical metanarrative with an ironic twist, for the idea that China represented a development solution to Africa was entertained first by European colonial officials. There were active colonial experiments with the idea that Chinese labour could assist with the 'opening up' of Africa – under European direction, of course.[5] With Chinese diplomats and businesses operating independently of European control throughout Africa, this script is being quite radically rewritten. Concerns with China's engagement in Africa today are evocative of a similar debate in the West during the 1960s, when the conjunction of decolonisation and expanding Red Chinese (not to mention Soviet) activity in Africa provoked fears in Western policy makers about the political impact of an Eastern ideological wind.

Today's unprecedented interest amongst the media, academic quarters, and a range of governments and international organisations evokes but exceeds the last comparable episode of attention, the wave of interest that followed Zhou En Lai's African political safari in 1963–64. That was a very different context: rather than revolutionary prospects being 'excellent', as Zhou infamously declared in Mogadishu, the FOCAC proclaimed this to be the case for China and Africa's 'new strategic partnership' for common prosperity. China's return is occurring under new circumstances. A more developed China operates under conditions of enhanced interdependence. Gone is the Soviet Union. Taiwan has lost the diplomatic recognition contest. Ideological disagreements have been superseded by political differences, especially on the key concept of sovereignty, as China participates in the global economy and pursues better trade terms rather than an alternative economic socialist vision. Practical Chinese engagement, including Chinese companies, is still facilitated by and anchored within a state framework. The array of Chinese in Africa is more diverse, however, with an increase in entrepreneurial migration including to such locations as Cape Verde.[6]

Why China in Africa matters

The first reason why China's return to Africa is important is that it is there to stay. With the addition of India and Asian states, this is part of what has been described as 'the most dramatic and important factor in the external relations of the continent – perhaps in the development of Africa as a whole – since the end of the Cold War'.[7] China's involvement in Africa waxed and waned in the post-colonial period and amidst the Cold War. Now, however, there is greater reason than ever before to suggest that more than an ephemeral phase, China's engagement with Africa will persist and deepen and that the present phase represents a departure from its past involvement. Observers considered that the PRC was in Africa to stay in the 1960s; some even dismissed its importance in Africa in the early 1990s. However, the context of relations has importantly altered. A progressively interdependent China, the future of whose Communist Party state is now more firmly linked to its performance at home, must continue to engage in order to guarantee essential supplies to maintain its development.

China needs, and will continue to need, African resources more than previously. One commentator wrote in the early 1970s: 'For the most part strategic minerals do not figure prominently in China's quest for economic relations with Africa.'[8] Today a fundamental aspect underpinning relations is modern China's need for a range of resources to supply its rising domestic and industrial needs. The most important sector by far is oil: some 30 per cent of China's oil comes from Africa, its top suppliers being Angola (14 per cent), Sudan (7 per cent) and Congo-Brazzaville (4.4 per cent). China's energy diplomacy (*nengyuan waijiao*) has mainstreamed as a foreign policy issue in the Hu Jintao period, which has seen an expansion and intensification of diplomacy not merely in Africa. 'An unprecedented need for resources is now driving China's foreign policy.'[9] The Chinese government's relationship-building diplomacy with oil states is a means to enhance its energy security.[10] Chinese national oil companies are pivotal drivers of overseas oil investment not just in extraction, but now also in exploration, as seen in recent agreements with Kenya or CNPC's current operations in Niger's Tenere oil block.

The second area of why China matters relates to increasing trade and investment in Africa, and the impact of this on political economy and for Africa's international relations. Sub-Saharan trade remains proportionally not as significant as its world trade but has grown rapidly and if sustained, 'the likely future impacts may be very substantial'.[11] Total trade for 2006, according to official statistics, is expected to be over US$450 billion, more than Africa–EU trade. This is spearheaded by the strategic pursuit of resources, around which investment is concentrated, and attempt to protect and enable a guaranteed flow of raw materials for China's energy needs. China's foreign direct investment for Africa as of mid-2006 of some US$41.18 billion is mostly channelled to resource-rich countries, headed by Sudan and Nigeria. As such, the thrust of China's relations can be considered as fundamentally extractive, with other motivating factors, such as Africa as a market or production platform, less important at this stage of relations. The growth in African exports is thus predominantly confined to a growth of major commodity exports to China and India.[12] China is contributing to an intensification of predominantly extractive economic activity reinforcing the existing unequal geographical distribution based on variable resource endowments. Resource-rich states like Angola, Nigeria, or Sudan are receiving most attention. Tellingly, over 50 per cent of Africa's exports to China come in the form of oil. Indeed, 85 per cent of Africa's exports to China come from five oil and mineral exporting countries.[13] As a developing power looking to grow within a globalising world, China has distinctive aspects in its African relations. However, it 'replicates in key ways developed state policies of disadvantageous terms of trade, exploitation of natural resources, oppressive labor regimes and support for authoritarian rulers. The commonalities of the PRC and Western approaches are therefore fundamental.'[14]

The political implications of this uneven geography of concentrated Chinese investment and economic activity are varied and context dependent rather than pre-determined, but also harder to assess than measurable trade flows. They are potentially most significant in resource-rich countries whose governance track records are not exemplary. Sudan is different from Botswana. The Chinese government's willingness to develop close political relations without overt governance conditionalities may in places work against those holding democratic commitments but is popular with regimes. Against this pattern of economic cooperation is a revival of 'triangulation' under new international circumstances, or situations where states are not dependent on one external patron but can pursue relations with two external states and can attempt to benefit politically or economically from competition and the greater room for manoeuvre this allows. As a means

Concerns with China's engagement in Africa today are evocative of a similar debate in the West during the 1960s, when the conjunction of decolonisation and expanding Red Chinese (not to mention Soviet) activity in Africa provoked fears in Western policy makers about the political impact of an Eastern ideological wind.

for governing elites in Africa to play off external patrons, triangulation was a feature of the Cold War, including China's relations with Africa (Tanzania, for example, was involved in relations with China and Sweden). This is a political possibility that has returned in parts of Africa. It was epitomised by Angola's turn to China as its negotiations with the IMF faltered in 2003 and China's rapid extension of a US$42 billion credit line a year later, which was backed up recently by an extra US$42 billion loan from the Export-Import Bank (ExIm) of China agreed during Premier Wen Jiabao's visit to Luanda in June 2006.

If China offers strategic potential for certain governing elites, there is also the potential for emerging geopolitical dynamics initiated by China's

---

*China's official development discourse
is explicitly non-prescriptive, employing
a language of 'no strings attached', equality
and mutual benefit. It emphasises the collective
right to development over the rights-based
approaches focused on individual rights.*

---

involvement throughout Africa and, specifically, the geopolitics of resource scarcity. Washington, not to mention former colonial European metropoles, watches with concern. Just as Africa is part of a broader Chinese foreign relations menu, China in Africa connects to larger global political dynamics.

A third area, albeit less significant for now, where China matters is its emerging development agenda in Africa and the considerable interest from different parts of Africa in applying aspects of China's development experience in their own contexts. China's legitimacy in questions of development rests in part on its own domestic record. It additionally benefits from a certain popular disillusionment with post-colonial development efforts in Africa, and the promise that China can deliver where 'the West' has not. China's official development discourse diverges: it is explicitly non-prescriptive, employing a language of 'no strings attached', equality and mutual benefit. It emphasises the collective right to development over the rights-based approaches focused on individual rights. It stresses the importance of political stability, internally-driven development appropriate to given conditions and promotes a sovereignty-based order. Finally, its non-intervention approach publicly separates business from politics.

China gains political capital from those areas where it diverges most from Western development prescriptions and associated conditionalities, coupled with its proven reputation for effective implementation of projects. The official Chinese approach works through and within existing political contours in Africa, rather than seeking to change these according to its own prescriptions and models. It challenges much development 'orthodoxy' on the relationship between development and democracy but the idea that there is a rival 'Beijing Consensus' is misleading, a construct applied to rather than emanating from China.[15] As it stands, the Chinese government seeks to strengthen its growing African relations through claims to legitimate development activity in Africa through a combination of common positions, including its support for the Millennium Development Goals, and differences; a development in Africa discourse with Chinese characteristics. The terms and practices of China as a donor remain opaque, with indications that private strings are attached. Beijing also likes to remind Western governments of their primary obligations for development in Africa. At times, the Chinese government has appeared to want to bandwagon on 'international' development efforts while also participating in development as a means to enhance claims to responsible world status, further aspirations to leadership of the developing world and benefit from resource extraction. After FOCAC, there are signs that it is intent on expanding development activity.

Normalising China–Africa relations

Through experience, familiarity, and the progressive deepening of links, Chinese actors are becoming a more established part of Africa. This process whereby a range of Chinese interests become a more normal part of life is one that must necessarily erode the popular reputation for exceptionalism China has enjoyed, together with such particular cases as Darfur. In the political imagery in different parts of Africa, projections of China are often made in these terms, especially during and after FOCAC, in keeping with the West's historic tendency to alternate between seeing China as a great hope or threat.

The first broad area where this process is set to proceed concerns the political implications – internal and international – of China's approach to political relations with African states and the limits of public adherence to non-interference. Giving a corporate marketing edge to a political position, one Chinese minister asserted: 'Nonintervention is our brand, like intervention is the Americans' brand.'[16] However, the idea of separate business and political realms is deeply disingenuous. The Chinese approach business as functional politics. The 'business, not politics' approach depends on an ability to navigate political waters, which will necessarily be enmeshed in politics and entail a logic of negotiation and conflict of a political (if not always openly so) nature. When it comes to protecting existing investments that have been established on the basis of political non-interference, China's African involvement is likely to need to evolve once the boundaries of its 'late-entry' non-interference mode of engagement are tested and transgressed. The public arguments during the 2006 Zambian presidential elections between opposition candidate Michael Sata and the response of the Chinese ambassador, threatening to cut aid if Sata won, illustrate one response made in the course of consolidating China's position in Zambia and protecting its investments.[17] At this point, it is too early to make generalisations about the impact on governance, or present Zimbabwe writ large as the future of the whole of a heterogeneous continent. The OECD, for example, point out, that 'transparency scores have not deteriorated during recent years when the presence of the Asian giants became more visible in Africa'.[18] However, it recognises that Africa's deepening reliance on commodity industries is not good for addressing poverty nor widening political representation.

A second point is the need to engage the Chinese side better and to appreciate the evolving challenges China faces domestically and in the international context as it pursues its own development. There are reasons to suggest that 'linear predictions of a manifest Chinese destiny may be flawed'.[19] Contextualising Africa within wider Chinese trade, foreign policy and participation in the global trade system, including the indirect impacts of China on Africa's economic performance, is important. China's trade with Africa is proportionally a small part (3 per cent) of its international trade and its energy needs are not neatly separable from those of global corporations (some of whom have invested in the Chinese oil majors operating in Africa).

There is the question of international responses. In the longer term China may reconfigure and could even break the monopoly of development concern and activity held by the current set of international organisations if its relations evolve to a deeper structural level of involvement. Ideas mooted about a Chinese Development Bank for Africa raises the question, for example, of how China may affect the international donor landscape of development finance in Africa. However, while keen to promote a range of development concerns, from aid, health, education, and even the environment, Beijing operates within prevailing international standards, including the Millennium Development Goals, and does not seek to challenge these. The competition China represents could catalyse new creative responses from the different layers of existing development architecture in Africa. 'Engaging' China on development issues in Africa will become a more normal part of work for more established development organisations as Chinese engagement deepens. The premise that through a variety of mechanisms from dialogue, cooperation, to institutional co-option, the Chinese

---

Can Africa benefit in the longer term,
in more sustainable and more representative ways
from China's enhanced attention and links with
Africa in a manner that departs from established
patterns with external powers?

---

state can be socialised into and accept the values espoused by the 'international' development system, underpin responses to date. Beyond such 'engagement', forms of dialogue and cooperation will also be necessary in what remains firmly anchored in a Chinese state framework

The final area concerns how different constituencies in Africa can respond. Can African governments develop appropriate responses and pursue these bilaterally, and also through more coordinated means through common positions via the AU? On the one hand, African governments can attempt to 'take the opportunity of the competition between China and the West and obtain the best terms for our people.'[20] On the other hand, many African governments face the challenge of how to maintain good relations with and yet not become economically and politically dependent on China. This relates to how mutually beneficial triangular relations can be productively managed to best benefit, which can entail retaining at least a degree of autonomy for action. In this, not just African states, but developed economies also face the need to respond to Chinese economic competition.

Beyond the state arena, the ability of African civil society groups – some of whom may, as seen in Zambia, seek to develop relations with China – to engage Chinese business, the Chinese state and their own governments effectively on issues of concern is a largely uncharted area.

Across a range of African contexts, China renews the problems and potential benefits of external intervention and what the Chinese will contribute in terms of lasting political and economic impact remains an open question. An illustration of this in practice is the future impact of Chinese lending to African countries on the back of debt relief. ExIm Bank is a state bank that appears to have rapidly become one of the largest export credit agencies but operates independently of prevailing export credit rules. A number of new African borrower countries with ExIm Bank, such as Ghana (projected US$41.2 billion new loans) and Mozambique (US$42.3 billion for the Mepanda Nkua dam and hydroelectric plan), were granted debt relief under the highly-indebted poor country initiative but while new loan terms are opaque, new lending could become a problem.[21] The Chinese rise in Africa poses particular problems for 'resource curse' scenarios and the perpetuation of the 'paradox of plenty'. Rather than establishing a new, illiberal 'Chinese' political economy of resource extraction, the current nature of China's expansion in Africa is more likely to deepen the existing political economy of natural resource extraction, especially in the oil sector.[22] Given the importance placed on infrastructure development by Chinese contractors, that this could facilitate more production-related investment and development of markets is one medium to longer term possibility for addressing unbalanced economic links.

Conclusion

China's return to African is a consequential subject that it is developing rapidly. However, despite wide coverage, not enough is known about concrete dynamics and significant knowledge gaps remain, including those exchanges that are less visible at present – commodity flows, education, the creation of new elites, or African business in China. Singling out an abstract 'China' in Africa has, of course, limited headline value and needs to be disaggregated to more properly reflect the dynamics of the Chinese engagement.

In such topical countries as Sudan, where Petronas and ONGC-Videsh are important together with CNPC, China is part of what is better approached as an Asian–African axis, the cumulative impact of which may be to effect a historic shift in the centre of political and economic gravity. However, as well as contextualising the seemingly meteoric rise of China in Africa, a historical approach would temper such crystal-ball gazing with caution about the limitations of long-term projects. Africa may have taken over Beijing during the 2006 FOCAC, but there is no inevitability about a transformative impact.

China bears a growing responsibility to match practice with its positive approach, to demonstrate it is different, rather than merely assert this with its official discourse which sets high standards and concomitant expectations of its official discourse. The issue of whether China can 'prosper where others have failed'[23] could be inverted: can Africa benefit in the longer term, in more sustainable and more representative ways from China's enhanced attention and links with Africa in a manner that departs from established patterns with external powers? Through a historical lens, China has set the terms of its African engagement up to and largely including the present; 'the onus rests upon African leaders to push the development agenda to the next level'.[24]

There is thus a need to retain perspective of relations as they currently stand, and not exaggerate the importance of China but at the same time to recognise that this is consequential and not ephemeral. The idea, for example, that '"Empire" has begun to die before our very eyes, and Beijing will be written on its heart!' may be indicative of current stratospheric hopes held in some quarters, but must be tempered. As President Nyerere recognised, while 'equality and mutual benefit' is a key tenet of relations, Tanzania–China relations was a partnership of 'most unequal equals', and this could also be used more generally to capture broader China–Africa relations.[25] At the end of China's Year of Africa, as the beginning of its return to African ends, and as it becomes a normal phenomenon throughout the continent, there are good reasons to contemplate a possible Chinese decade of Africa. While there are cautious signs at this more optimistic stage that new relations could bring potentially beneficial aspects, ultimately, and away from official state relations showcased at the FOCAC, China's re-engagement reprises questions of power, states and constraints on development, includ-

ing Africa's unfavourable position in the world market, that are sadly familiar in Africa's post-colonial history. Those with high hopes that China can
benefit Africa as well as itself, for example, have to recognise its current economic involvement must change for broader development to occur. Besides
today's optimism in many quarters, there is also disenchantment in Africa
with the impact of China's business activity and linked international diplomacy. As a Darfurian, summing up a personal cycle in his own relationship
to China from the 1970s and now, said: 'As Darfurians, we used to love
China. We read the Quran and we read the Red Book...I used to be biased
in favour of them, now I am biased against them.'[26] Once the dust settles
on the current China-in-Africa fever, and notions of China's exceptionalism
wear off, all involved will need to harness hopes to realistic vehicles in order
to make the most of the current potential.

*Daniel Large is a doctoral research student at the School of Oriental and African
Studies, London and has studied in China and conducted research in Africa. He is
co-editing a book on China-Africa relations to be published early in 2007.*

Notes

1 As observed by Maurice Gountin, who experienced both, during his presentation 'China's
assistance to Africa, a stone bridge of Sino-Africa relations', China-Africa Links workshop,
Center on China's Transnational Relations, The Hong Kong University of Science and
Technology, 11 November 2006.

2 To rephrase, slightly, a comment by the Chinese Emperor in 1415. J.J. L. Duyvendak (1949)
China's Discovery of Africa. London: Arthur Probsthain, 33.

3 For a systematic account, see Chris Alden (2006) 'China-Africa Relations: the end of the
beginning', in Peter Draper and Garth le Pere, eds, *Enter the Dragon: Towards a Free Trade
Agreement between China and the Southern African Customs Union*. Midrand: Institute for Global
Dialogue/South African Institute for International Affairs, 137–153.

4 The Forum for Economic Cooperation and Trade between China and the Portuguese
Speaking Countries.

5 See Philip Snow (1988) *The Star Raft: China's Encounter with Africa*. London: Weidenfeld and
Nicolson, for historical background.

6 See Heidi Haugen and Jorgen Carling (2005) 'On the edge of the Chinese diaspora: The
surge of baihuo business in an African city', *Ethnic and Racial Studies*, 28(4) 639–662.

7 Christopher Clapham (2006) 'Fitting China in', paper delivered at the conference 'A "Chinese Scramble"? The Politics of Contemporary China-Africa Relations', Sidney Sussex College, Cambridge, 13 July.

8 Bruce D. Larkin (1971) *China and Africa 1949–1970: The Foreign Policy of the People's Republic of China*. Berkeley: University of California Press, 93.

9 David Zweig and Bi Jianhai (2005) 'China's Global Hunt for Energy', *Foreign Affairs* 84(5) 25.

10 Erica S. Downs (2004) 'The Chinese Energy Security Debate', *The China Quarterly*, 177, 21–41.

11 Raphael Kaplinsky, Dorothy McCormick, Mike Morris (2006) 'The Impact of China on Sub-Saharan Africa' (April 2006).

12 See Andrea Goldstein, Nicolas Pinaud et al (2006) 'China and India: What's in it for Africa?' OECD.

13 Harry G. Broadman (2007) *Africa's Silk Road: China and India's New Economic Frontier*. Washington: The World Bank, 12.

14 Barry Sautman, 'Friends and Interests: China's Distinctive Links with Africa' (2006) *Center on China's Transnational Relations Working Paper* no. 12, Hong Kong University of Science and Technology, 5.

15 One area where there should be consensus is the importance, amongst other things, of a flexible approach. 'I well remember Deng [Xiao Ping] telling the visiting president of Ghana, Jerry Rawlings, in September 1985: "Please don't copy our model. If there is any experience on our part, it is to formulate policies in light of one's own conditions."' Wei-Wei Zhang (2006) 'The allure of the Chinese model', *International Herald Tribune*, 1 November.

16 Jonathan Katzenellenbogen (2006) 'China Lays Out Red Carpet for Continent's Leaders', *Business Day*, 1 November.

17 A different example of China in Africa becoming a domestic political issue was seen in 1906 when Chinese labour in South Africa was a contentious domestic issue in the UK general election and the Liberal party made much of 'Chinese slavery in a British colony'.

18 Andrea Goldstein, Nicolas Pinaud et al (2006) 'China and India: What's in it for Africa?', OECD.

19 James Kynge (2006) *China Shakes the World: The Rise of a Hungry Nation*. London: Weidenfeld & Nicolson, 34.

20 (2006) 'Thinking Through Sino-Africa Relations', *Daily Trust* (Abuja), 13 November.

21 Todd Moss and Sarah Rose (2006) 'China ExIm Bank and Africa: New Lending, New Challenges', CGD Notes, November.

22 Ricardo Soares de Oliveira (2006) 'The Geopolitics of Chinese Oil Investment in Africa',

paper delivered at the conference 'A "Chinese Scramble"? The Politics of Contemporary China-Africa Relations', Sidney Sussex College, Cambridge, 12 July.

23 Eleneus Akanga, 'Can China prosper where others have failed?' (2006) *The New Times* (Kigali), 5 November.

24 Sanusha Naidu and Lucy Corkin (2006) 'Who was the real winner in China', *Business Day*, 9 November.

25 Speech in China in 1968. See George T. Yu (1970) *China and Tanzania: A Study in Cooperative Interaction*. Berkeley: Center for Chinese Studies, University of California.

26 Interview with El Khadir Daloum (2005) Nairobi, 29 November.

USEFUL LINKS AND RESOURCES

Official China websites

People's Daily online in English <http://english.people.com.cn/>
Official website of China-Africa summit <http://english.focacsummit.org/>
Xinhua News Agency website in English <http://news.xinhuanet.com/english/>
Chinese embassy in South Africa <http://www.chinese-embassy.org.za/>

Unofficial and semi-official sites

Afroshanghai.com: the African community in Shanghai and China is a Shanghai-based website and blog for African and Afro-American expats in China <http://www.afroshanghai.com/>
China Digital Times.net is 'a collaborative news website covering China's social and political transition and its emerging role in the world. ... Our goal is to harness the distributive power of the Internet to advance the world's understanding of China ... China's democratic transition, sustainable development and peaceful emergence in the global community'. It is run by the Berkeley China Internet Project in the Graduate School of Journalism at the University of California, Berkeley < http://chinadigitaltimes.net>
chinadialogue: China and the world discuss the environment is edited by Isabel Hilton and based in London and Beijing. It describes itself as 'the world's first fully bilingual website devoted to the environment'. With a joint British-Chinese board, it is part-financed by the UK government as part a series of 'sustainable development dialogues' (see http://www.sustainable-development.gov.uk/international/dialogues/) <http://www.chinadialogue.net/>

Business and economy

China Business – the special China section of the Hong Kong-based Asia Times Online <http://www.atimes.com/atimes/China_Business.html>
Business Report – South Africa <http://www.busrep.co.za/>

Thinktanks and news services

African Geopolitics 'world leaders and international experts express their views on African affairs'; 'the first bilingual quarterly on African affairs' <http://www.african-geopolitics.org/home_english.htm and also http://www.african-geopolitics.org/home_french.htm>
The Jamestown Foundation's 'mission is to inform and educate policy makers and the broader policy community about events and trends in those societies which are strategically or tactically important to the United States and which frequently restrict access to such information' <http://www.jamestown.org/>
Africa Confidential is one of the longest-established specialist publications on Africa, with a considerable reputation for being first with the in-depth news on significant political, economic and security developments across the continent: 'all our contributors write for us on the basis of strict anonymity, a principle that was established from the outset in 1960 to ensure writers' personal safety in the turbulent, early years of post-colonial African independence. Hence the newsletter's title' <http://www.africa-confidential.com/index.aspx?pageid=3>
Open Democracy 'is the leading independent website on global current affairs ... offering stimulating, critical analysis, promoting dialogue and debate on issues of global importance and linking citizens from around the world ... openDemocracy is committed to human rights and democracy' <http://www.opendemocracy.net/home/index.jsp>

Campaigns and NGOs

Global Witness 'campaigns to achieve real change by challenging established thinking on seemingly intractable global issues. We work to highlight the link between the exploitation of natural resources and human rights abuses, particularly where the resources such as timber, diamonds and oil are used to fund and perpetuate conflict and corruption' <http://www.globalwitness.org/>

Extractive Industries Transparency Initiative (EITI) supports improved governance in resource-rich countries through the full publication and verification of company payments and government revenues from oil, gas and mining campaigns <http://www.eitransparency.org/>

Human Rights Watch is dedicated to protecting the human rights of people around the world. 'We stand with victims and activists to prevent discrimination, to uphold political freedom, to protect people from inhumane conduct in wartime, and to bring offenders to justice' <http://www.hrw.org/>

Friends of the Earth defends the planet and champions a healthy and just world. Active in 70 countries, Friends of the Earth has the world's largest network of environmental groups <http://www.foe.org/>

Global Timber 'provides information and statistics on the global trade in wood-based products, especially that from Africa and East Asia [and] insights into trade in illegal timber particularly in relation to importing countries such as Japan, the UK, and the USA' <http://www.globaltimber.org.uk/>

Reuters Foundation – alerting humanitarians to emergencies <http://www.alertnet.org/>

Special issues

'China in Africa', special issue of the *South African Journal of International Affairs*, 13(10) Summer–Autumn 2006, ISSN: 1022-0461. See also the institute's website at www.saiia.org.za

Leni Wild and David Mepham (eds) (2006) *The New Sinosphere – China in Africa*. London: Institute for Public Policy Research, £9.95, ISBN 1 86030 302 1. See also the IPPR website at www.ippr.org

Podcasts

'Africa's relationship with China', Professor Kwesi Kwaa Prah speaks to Pambazuka News about the history of Chinese engagement in Africa and theorises about what is to come. This accompanies our special issue exploring China's relationship with Africa. Professor Kwaa Prah is about to release a book entitled *Afro-Chinese Relations: Past, Present and the Future*. He is based at the Centre for Advanced Studies of African Society. The music in this podcast is by Freddy Macha <http://www.pambazuka.org/en/broadcasts/index.php>

ABOUT PAMBAZUKA NEWS

Pambazuka News, founded in December 2000, has become one of the principal forums for debate, discussion, analysis and dissemination of information about social justice in Africa. It is distributed weekly as an e-newsletter and is also available free online at www.pambazuka.org. There are currently more than 40,000 articles, news and information entries on the online database, containing all the information published in the nearly 300 issues of the newspletter. In 2006, Pambazuka News began producing multimedia materials, including short audio ('podcasts') and video programmes that we distribute via the internet.

Pambazuka News has been widely used by civil society organisations, coalitions and alliances for advocacy and campaigning, and has contributed significantly to the campaign on the Protocol on the Rights of Women in Africa led by Solidarity for African Women's Rights (SOAWR).

Pambazuka News is published by Fahamu (for details see below) with the support of Christian Aid, the Ford Foundation, the New Field Foundation Fund of the Tides Foundation, TrustAfrica and many individual donors. Fahamu also receives support for the production of books and special issues of Pambazuka News from HIVOS, OXFAM GB, and the Sigrid Rausing Trust.

About Fahamu

Fahamu, a not-for-profit organisation founded in 1997, has a vision of the world where people organise to emancipate themselves from all forms of oppression, recognise their social responsibilities, respect each other's differences, and realise their full potential.

Fahamu supports human rights and social justice in Africa through the innovative use of information and communications technologies, stimulating debate, discussion and analysis, distributing news and information, and developing training materials and running distance-learning courses. Fahamu focuses primarily on Africa, although we work with others to support the global movement for human rights and social justice.

Fahamu has developed a wide range of courses for human rights organisations, including courses on investigating and reporting on human rights violations, conflict prevention, prevention of torture, fundraising, financial management and others. Fahamu's distance-learning methodology, involving CDROMs, email-based facilitation and workshops, has been widely used in collaboration with institutions such as the University of Oxford, Office of the UN High Commissioner for Human Rights, Article 19, the UN-affiliated University for Peace and others. For further details see www. fahamu.org.

Lightning Source UK Ltd.
Milton Keynes UK
UKOW041828160413

209343UK00001B/202/A